Vots

expert gardening guide

create your own

edible
garden

Collins

Published by Collins
An imprint of HarperCollins Publishers
Westerhill Road, Bishopbriggs, Glasgow G64 2QT
www.harpercollins.co.uk
collins.reference@harpercollins.co.uk

HarperCollins Publishers
1st Floor, Watermarque Building, Ringsend Road,
Dublin 4, Ireland

A catalogue record for this book is available from
the British Library

ISBN 978-0-00-846114-0

10 9 8 7 6 5 4 3 2 1

Printed in Slovenia by GPS Group

Thanks to my agents, Charlotte Robertson and
Debbie Scheisse, and everyone at HarperCollins
Publishers including Gerry Breslin, Gordon
MacGilp, Lauren Murray and Kevin Robbins.

Photo credits
page 62 © Matthew Taylor / Alamy Stock
Photo; page 85 © Deborah Vernon / Alamy
Stock Photo; page 90 © anna quaglia / Alamy
Stock Photo; pages 108-109 © Food and
Drink Photos / Alamy Stock Photo; page 165 ©
blickwinkel/McPHOTO/H.-R. Mueller / Alamy
Stock Photo; page 181 © Nigel Cattlin / Alamy
Stock Photo; page 187 (middle) © Sally Mundy
/ Alamy Stock Photo; page 188 (top) © Manfred
Habel / Alamy Stock Photo; page 196 (top right)
© Richard Becker / Alamy Stock Photo

All other images © Shutterstock.com

Joe's

expert gardening guide

create your own

edible
garden

introduction

the basics

vegetables

fruit

care

glossary

index

Introduction

Eating something that you've grown yourself is one of life's greatest pleasures. The joy and satisfaction lie in the simple process of sowing a seed, nurturing it, picking the produce and tasting it; a fundamental, humbling and wonderful experience that connects one to the wider world. If you grow your own, you also know precisely where that food has come from and what's gone into it. If you are an organic gardener, it gives you complete control using those simple and effective methods.

The taste of freshly picked home-grown produce can be noticeably superior to shop-bought. They may not be quite as uniform in size and shape but ultimately, it's all about the taste and eating something in season, rather than it being flown halfway round the world and still not being that tasty!

Some gardeners start off growing ornamental plants in their gardens, then move on to edibles. Many get hooked and dig up their roses for more growing space, yet most find a happy balance between the two within their gardens. Some will take on an allotment as I did and there are an increasing number of community gardens and shared spaces for people to grow their own in. These can be wonderful places to socialise and share tips and knowledge of growing fruit and veg. Then there are those that have a tiny outside area – perhaps no soil at all to dig into – yet still manage to grow a good range and decent quantity of crops in pots and containers.

Anyone who has children knows how difficult it can be to get them to eat their five a day. Involving them even on a small scale can be transformative as it's fun and engaging and they'll want to eat or at least try something out if they've cultivated it themselves. It also educates youngsters into understanding where food actually comes from (not in packets from the supermarket!) and often opens up discussions on the wider issues of food security, sustainability and the environment. My kids loved our allotment; we have many fabulous and enduring memories from those days gardening together.

There is perhaps a little mystique around growing edibles? Does one have to be 'green fingered', have lots of experience and ideally know some magic tricks? There are serious competitive growers out there who might want to grow the biggest or the most perfect looking but most of us just want to grow something tasty. The good news is that most edibles are extremely easy to grow, we just have to follow a few basics and tune ourselves in with the soil and the seasons. We've all had and will continue to have both successes and failures along the way (as my mother-in-law says, 'if you've never put a fork through a potato, then you've never dug up a potato'!) but they are all learning experiences and make us all better gardeners in the long run.

Start off small, grow what you love to eat and enjoy!

the basics

Planning a veggie patch

My advice is to start small and don't get over-ambitious. One large planting area approximately 1.2 m x 4 m is adequate to start off with. With succession sowing throughout the season, it could produce plenty: some fresh salads, French beans, tomatoes, courgettes, potatoes, spring onions, radishes, pak choi, etc. You could go far smaller than that and if you don't have any soil you can still grow plenty in containers and pots or make some raised beds.

Choosing a site

Most edibles prefer plenty of sun and a free-draining fertile soil. Poor topsoil can be significantly improved (see below), but in an ideal world try to choose an area that has good-quality free-draining topsoil already. Avoid shady or dry areas next to buildings, walls and fences or under trees to site your vegetable patch. Easy access all the way round is important too for sowing, weeding and watering, so try not to block yourself off.

Lifting turf and shaping planting beds

Once you have an idea of where to site your vegetable garden, you can start marking out the shapes of the planting areas. Use pegs and some string to lay them out, keeping the shapes practical so you can reach every part without standing on the soil. The accepted width of an allotment bed is 1.2 m (so you can reach the middle from both sides) and around 2.4 m to 3.0 m long to stop the temptation to cut across the corners. You may want to put down a simple path between them. The cheapest method is to pin down some landscape fabric onto the soil (use thick galvanised wire bent into 'U' pins) and then spread some bark chips over the top. Make sure the path is wide enough for a barrow if you're planning to use one.

If your soil is good quality, simply remove the turf or existing plants in the way and dig over. You may want to install some more permanent edging, using treated gravel boards and pegs that will also bring the level up a few centimetres, ideal to introduce a thick layer of mulch (see below).

Soil preparation

The amount of work needed to get your ground-level soil into shape depends on your soil type, what you intend to grow and how well it has been cultivated in the past. Single digging to one spit (a spade's depth) and incorporating plenty of organic matter is usually enough for most crops but on very heavy soil or if you want to grow beans, peas and potatoes, then consider double digging (digging to two spits' depth).

New ground

Heavy clay and new ground can be dug over and left in large clods for the frosts to break up for you over the winter. It's unlikely that very rough ground will be of good enough quality by next spring for the smaller and more fiddly seedlings, so consider planting potatoes in it for the first year. They are the ideal crop on rough ground and the soil gets dug during planting, earthing up and harvesting to break it up even more, so by the end of the season has usually been broken to a fine tilth.

organic matter

Autumn is the perfect time to add as thick a layer as possible of organic matter as a mulch onto planting areas or raised beds, as the worms will work it into the soil over the winter. Well-rotted horse manure, garden compost, council compost and mushroom compost (slightly alkaline so good for brassicas) will all significantly improve your soil; their fibrous texture retains moisture while adding nutrients too.

Understanding your soil

Pick some up and play with it in your hand, it'll tell you almost everything you need to know except its pH, which can be tested using a simple testing kit.

A **clay soil** will feel lumpy and sticky when wet. It is made up of extremely fine particles. When it's dry it goes hard, and it will also drain poorly. Although it's hard to dig, if you work in plenty of compost and improve the drainage with grit or sharp sand it will make a good soil as it's high in nutrients. Clay soil warms up slowly in spring.

A **sandy soil** will be gritty to the touch as it is made up of larger particles which means that it's free-draining, easy to work and will warm up quickly in spring. The downside of this is that it will dry out rapidly in the summer and the nutrients wash through it when it rains so it will need plenty of organic matter adding on a regular basis to help retain moisture and feed the plants.

A **silty soil** will feel smooth to the touch and can be a fabulous soil if managed as it's free-draining but also retains moisture and is higher in nutrients than a sandy soil. As it's made up of fine particles it can get compacted easily but plenty of organic matter will help to keep the soil structure open and in top condition.

Peaty soils will be dark in colour and feel spongy if squeezed and will hold plenty of moisture. They are acidic and high in organic matter but low in nutrient levels. A peaty soil may need drainage improvement and can make a fabulous soil for certain plants if nutrients are added.

Chalky soil will be alkaline, stony and free-draining as it often overlays a chalk or limestone bedrock. Minerals such as iron and manganese will quickly leach out of the soil, but this can be remedied to a degree by regularly adding fertiliser.

The perfect soil type is **Loamy soil**, which is easy to work, and if you squeeze a handful it will hold together, but not stick like clay. It will warm up quickly in spring and both hold moisture and drain well too. If your garden is on loam, then think yourself lucky!

A quick and easy way to test the draining is to get a watering can and water an area of soil. If the surface water disappears quickly you're probably on a sandy or gravelly soil, but if it sits for a while you're probably on clay.

to dig or not to dig?

When I first started gardening, 'double digging' was seen as the 'correct' way to get your soil into the ideal state, especially for a veggie garden. This involved digging an entire trench to a spade's depth then breaking up the soil at the bottom with a fork, incorporating plenty of organic matter and then covering it with the topsoil from the next trench as you go – a laborious task. I know a few (admittedly old-school) gardeners who still carry out the ancient tradition, but they are a rare breed. Some dig pits using this method for their runner beans, which are particularly hungry plants.

Sure, it makes it light and manageable but too much air can degrade the soil structure, kill off important micro-organisms including beneficial soil fungi; in short, the good stuff. This in turn reduces fertility and moisture retention, which defeats the object as that's what we're aiming for in the first place.

Fantastic news I hear some of you say as you head back to the sofa with a cup of tea. Well, yes and no. The key is that whether you choose to dig or not, in the long run you need to get your soil into decent shape to start with, which usually means workable, weed-free, well drained, well manured, and so, more often than not, initially dug too.

No dig

Many gardeners swear by the 'no dig' approach. It's not altogether new and was being discussed and written about in the 1940s. The organic gardener Charles Dowding, a renowned and highly respected grower,

has been implementing 'no dig' for nearly 40 years and recording an experiment since 2007 with hugely successful results, which prove that it is possible to have higher yields and super healthy crops with less work.

Here's the basics

Materials needed: (1) plenty of organic matter; and (2) plenty of light-excluding material, such as cardboard (with all plastic labels and staples taken out).

- First, cut down or mow tall weed foliage to ground level.

- Place a layer of light-excluding material (cardboard, etc.) so the ground is completely covered. Make sure to overlap the gaps so no light can get through at all. Don't use carpet as most are treated with chemicals and dyes that can leach poisons onto the soil.

- Place a deep layer of mulch on top of the cardboard where you want your beds to go. Think about being able to reach plants without standing on the beds, ever! (1.2 metres is usually a maximum dimension to reach to the middle from both sides.)

- For the mulch, use homemade compost, fully rotted manure, leaves, straw, grass mowings, or even a mix of them all, so long as it is more than 15–20 cm thick

- You may want some paths that can simply be defined by another material (bark chippings? gravel?) or simply left for now as exposed cardboard.

- Tread it down firmly. Wait for six months for the weeds to die down and the soil organisms to do their work. It can take up to a year to kill off the weeds, especially pernicious ones like bindweed and bramble.

For an area that is already cultivated:

- Without digging it over, apply 15 cm minimum (ideally a bit more) of an organic, well-decomposed mulch to your beds. Worms will digest it and take it down, creating a rich and well-textured soil.

- Firm it by hand but don't overly compact it.

- You can immediately plant or sow (depending on the time of year) directly into this surface compost.

- Weeds will be easy to pull out from the soft surface. The soil beneath will be firm but not compacted and the soil organisms will form a network of air passages that are ideal for young plants to get their roots into.

- Every year, apply around 5 cm of compost or manure, ideally in spring after crops have been cleared, or in spring if the area has had winter crops growing on it.

weeds

The vast majority of allotment holders will tell you that weeds are their biggest problem, but wherever you grow your veggies, it is important to get on top of them and keep on top of them. Weeds compete for nutrients and moisture and, if left to their own devices, will quickly colonise areas of soil and smother crops. The first thing to do is to identify what sort of weeds you have, to know how to deal with them. Exactly what sort of weeds you get in your garden or allotment will depend to some extent on what sort of growing conditions you have.

Annual weeds

These germinate and mature in one season and die away, leaving a supply of seed to germinate in the autumn or the following season. The seeds can lie in your soil for over 30 years and still germinate when they come to the surface, so you'll never eliminate them altogether. It's important to keep on top of them and remove them before they get a chance to set seed, but the good news is that they can usually be hoed over and left on top of the soil, ideally on a hot day, where they will dry out and die off immediately. Job done.

Annual weeds include: groundsel, common field-speedwell, chickweed and sow thistle, among others.

perennial weeds

Perennial weeds are far trickier customers as they will spread by seed, but also by creeping stems and invasive root systems  that will regrow if damaged or part left in the ground. It's important with perennial weeds that you dig out the whole of the plant with a fork or daisy grubber. Sometimes it's completely impossible and some will be left in the ground to regenerate. Just keep on top of them at every opportunity and they will get weaker and weaker over time.

Perennial weeds include: bindweed, ground elder, couch grass, dandelions and creeping buttercup.

Brambles around the edge of a plot may give you a fine crop of blackberries but are best kept away from other plants. The best way to rid a plot of brambles is to strim them to the ground and dig their roots out with a sharp spade or mattock.

composting weeds

Most weeds are fine to put on the compost heap, but try to spot a pernicious root, which is best kept off altogether in my opinion. Seedheads should be kept off the compost heap. They can be sealed into a plastic bag using a rubber band and left on the top of the heap for a few weeks where the heat and lack of air will rot

them and make them unviable, so they won't come back.
Remember the old adage too: one year's seeding means
seven years' weeding so don't allow your weeds to set
seed. If they're right on the cusp of dispersal, walk round
with a paper bag and snap off the seedheads into the bag
before you do the dispersal all over your plot for them
when you pull them out!

covering areas

Weeds can only grow where there is moisture and light.
If you have an area of ground in the garden or allotment
and you have time, consider covering the entire area
with a landscape fabric or black plastic sheeting to
exclude light. Mow or strim it first and perhaps (ideal
but not essential) spread a layer of compost or similar
first that will break down and improve the soil in the
process. Weight or peg it down so it doesn't blow away.
Ideally, place it in late winter as many weeds will die in
the spring flush. The longer you leave it the better, but
a minimum of two or three months in spring/summer
or six months over winter. Once lifted, there may still
be some perennial weeds but they should be weak and
easier to dig out. Cardboard and newspapers can also be
used by themselves (but need more pegging down) or as
a supplement beneath the other covering (see 'No dig' in
the previous section).

Flame gun

These are effective and popular for gravel areas, areas
with no plants perhaps when clearing initially and paths,
as the powerful ones burn weeds right down to the roots
without the need for chemicals. Of course, they come
with safety notes!

mulching

Regular mulching on growing areas (with compost/
well-rotted horse manure/mushroom compost; see the
planning a veggie patch section) not only improves the
soil and moisture retention but will smother annual
weeds and seeds too.

using weedkillers

I wouldn't use any chemical weedkillers on any areas
where edibles are to be grown. There is an increasing
range of organic weedkillers that contain ingredients
like fatty acids, vinegar or acetic acid, and essential
oils (eugenol, clove oil, citrus oil). They are particularly
effective on small young annual weeds (the ones that are
easy to hoe out anyway).

raised beds

Raised beds can create the ideal growing conditions for a wide range of edibles. They can be quite a lot of work to make but, for some sites, are ideal and well worth the investment of time and money.

Advantages

- They drain very well so are ideal if your soil gets waterlogged.

- Can be built directly on top of poor soil areas (heavy clay or unfertile) as well as directly on any hard surfaces in the garden or allotment without the need for removing them first.

- They reduce soil compaction as the planting area is never stepped on, which means the plants' roots get plenty of air, which encourages fast growth.

- Compost and fertiliser can be added more accurately.

- The soil warms up quicker in spring so plants can be sown and cropped earlier.

- They help to organise the overall planting strategy and crops are easily changed from year to year.

- They are easy to garden as they are at an accessible height, which means less bending over.

- They bring planting higher and therefore help to visually make more impact, especially in a small garden.

- You can choose what type of soil you want in them. If your garden soil is particularly acidic or alkaline, you can have a contrasting soil or neutral soil to increase your range of edibles.

- Plants can be grown close together as you don't need paths or spaces to tread. Don't be tempted to overplant though as they tend to grow larger in raised beds anyway due to the optimum conditions.

- Raised beds can easily be covered with a cloche to increase the growing season at both ends (sowing earlier and harvesting later).

How to make

The depth of a raised bed all depends on what you want to grow and how high you want them for ideal access (root veggies like parsnips need a deep root run). Anywhere between 15 cm minimum to around 50 cm works well.

Of course, the higher they get the more material and soil you'll need to make and fill them with. On top of a hard surface, look for a minimum depth of 45 cm as they can drain too freely if shallower. For veggies, a width of 1.2 m means you can access the middle from both sides; any wider will be too much of a stretch.

Materials

Brick or concrete blocks offer a permanent solution but they will need foundations and can get expensive.

- New railway sleepers are heavy, stack on top of each other and can be screwed together using specific (timberlock) screws and rarely need wooden posts to support them.

- A cheaper material is timber gravel boards or reclaimed scaffold boards, which will need the support of timber posts (driven or concreted into the ground) but are great on the allotment or for less permanent beds.

- Brick or concrete blocks offer a permanent solution but they will need foundations and can get expensive. You may want them anyway, to tie in with the aesthetics of your garden?

I always line the inside walls of a timber raised bed using some heavy-duty plastic sheet or landscape fabric pinned just below the top, so you don't see it. This keeps the soil away from the wood, stopping it from rotting and increasing the lifespan.

I don't usually line the bottom unless there is a major weed problem (mare's tail, bindweed). I would then use some landscape fabric on the bottom of the raised bed covering all the soil to create a barrier between the new soil and the ground. Water can get through the fabric, but the weeds will be suppressed.

If heavily compacted, fork over the soil beneath before backfilling. The soil and compost mix you choose to backfill with will depend on what you want to grow but for most plants I'd go for a mix of loamy soil and add in plenty of compost or well-rotted manure. Just using compost alone will be too free-draining and won't retain enough moisture.

crop rotation

Growing the same crop in the same spot year on year can lead to a build-up of soil-dwelling pests and diseases and the level of nutrients often becomes unbalanced too. Rotating crops helps break the cycle of pest and disease build-up, keep the soil healthy and helps to organise your crops for their cultivation needs too.

Some gardeners create extremely complicated crop rotation strategies and charts (sometimes for large patches or smallholdings). I'd rather keep it simple! If in any doubt, just avoid growing the same annual crop in the same place two years in a row.

Here's a simple three-year rotation you can follow:

3 year crop Rotation

| Root
& Bulb | Fruit
& Seed | Leaf
& Stem |

If you want to step it up to a four-year rotation, dividing the beds up into potatoes, legumes, brassicas and roots will work nicely.

Everyone likes to grow different vegetables and you may not include them all in your choices, so here are some other basic principles worth adhering to for success:

- Potatoes do best in a rich soil, slightly on the acidic side, so add manure before planting potatoes.

- Root crops such as carrots and parsnips prefer soil that hasn't been manured the previous autumn as it can make them fork and split. They tend to like a light soil on the alkaline side so lime (in the form of 'garden lime', calcified seaweed or ground chalk at the recommended dose) can be added if the pH is low.

- Beetroots and onions don't need rich soil so can fit with the roots in a rotation if needed.

- Legumes (peas and beans) like manure and rich soils. They take nitrogen from the air and store it in their roots (called nitrogen fixing). This nitrogen-rich soil is ideal for growing brassicas so these often follow legumes in the rotation cycle.

- Where possible, keep plants of the same family together as their requirements will be similar.

- Crops like lettuce, cut-and-come-again salad leaves and cucurbits (cucumber, courgette, pumpkin and squash, etc.) will work wherever there's a space for them.

comfrey

Symphytum officinale, commonly known as comfrey, is a special plant and essential if you're getting serious about growing edibles. The best variety to get is one called Bocking 14. It's sterile so won't produce seeds that will germinate all over the place. It does spread and thicken up very quickly and will produce great patches of invaluable foliage. It is tolerant of sun, partial shade and can be grown in pretty deep shade. It prefers soil with at least some moisture in it and will take off in damp soils.

Once you have it, you'll have it for a long time so do consider where to plant it. Bocking 14 doesn't set seed but if you dig it up and leave any piece of root in the soil, it will grow into a new plant. So, what's the big deal with comfrey?

- It's the best stuff to add loads of nutrients to a compost heap. Its roots go down deep and drag up nutrients, especially potassium, and this ends up in the leaves of the plant. When you put the leaves on the compost heap, they rot down and release the nutrients into the mix.

- Still in the compost heap, comfrey leaves actually speed up the rotting process. That's because the richness of the leaves – and it's a natural richness – encourages the bacterial and fungal activity to move on quickly.

- It can be used neat, cut straight off the plant and placed directly into planting trenches (ideal for potatoes). As the leaves rot down, they provide essential nutrients.

- Chopped leaves can be used directly as a mulch that aids water retention (and again will slowly release nutrients around the plants).

- Comfrey leaves can be soaked in water to create a fantastic liquid feed. Gardening isn't an exact science but making comfrey feed is a kind of chemistry. Get yourself some leaves, put them in an old dustbin or bucket, fill up with water, cover (and this is advisable – trust me) and wait for four weeks. Try and fill whatever the container is up to a quarter with leaves and the rest topped up with water. This stuff stinks to high heaven as it rots.

- Then all you have to do is dip some into your watering can and water your plants. It's potassium rich so particularly effective with encouraging flowering and fruit setting for plants like tomatoes and runner beans.

composting

The compost heap is the garden's engine room. The compost itself, when added into your soil will make it fertile, moisture-retentive and nutrient rich – the very basis of a healthy garden.

It's easy to make as long as you get a few basics right.

making a compost heap

There are many products around and some councils will supply or subsidise a compost bin. Ideally, it will be big enough for the amount of waste your garden (and house) produces, or you could get two, or even three! You can make one out of old pallets and make it easy to access from the front, and ideally line it with old pieces of wood or cardboard. Make a lid out of plastic sheeting or old carpet to keep heat in.

siting your compost heap

Place it in sun or semi-shade and directly onto soil if possible, so insects can get in and help break it down. Sun heats the compost and speeds up the process. Screen it from key views with plants or trellising.

what to put on it

The best proportion is 50/50 of 'green' and 'brown' materials mixed together.

Greens include vegetable peelings, leaf material from plants, grass clippings (in layers and not too much at once), nettles, annual weeds, comfrey, tea bags and coffee grounds.

Browns include cardboard, cardboard tubes, shredded paper (including glossy magazines), woody materials, hay, straw, sawdust, wood shavings, hedge clippings and fallen leaves. Other good materials include eggshells, 100% natural clothes/fibres and wood ash in moderation.

what not to put on it

Avoid pernicious weeds such as bindweed, horsetail, or weeds with seedheads that may increase your weeding problem in the future. Don't put meat, fish or cooked food, as these may attract vermin.

making the compost

Look to mix between green and browns as you go, avoiding large layers of one or the other and chop up any tough flower stems with a spade on the ground before adding. Water once in place. Not too wet, not too dry, just lightly moist (think baking a cake!). Keep it covered and the heap should warm up. Frequent turning makes better and quicker compost; once a month is ideal. Compost can be made in eight weeks (by the compost ninjas) but it usually takes around a year on average. It should be non-smelly, dark and crumbly. Don't worry if it isn't absolutely perfect and is a bit lumpy or has the odd twig or unbroken-down leaf in it, it'll still work.

green manures

When a plant is harvested, and the top growth of a plant is removed, nutrients that were in the soil are taken with it. If left to die back naturally, those nutrients would be returned into the soil. Green manures are fast-growing crops that get dug back into the soil to feed whatever's going in next. Many can get their roots down so pull up and harness those nutrients that can't be accessed by other crops, which are then fed back into the soil (when dug in) at a more accessible level.

Their leaves also add in bulky organic matter (good for soil structure and moisture retention) and those sown in autumn help reduce nutrients getting washed away by winter rains. Summer-grown green manures (such as fenugreek or buckwheat) carpet the ground and suppress weeds. Many also look great when they flower and encourage beneficial insects.

Green manures are best used in distinct clear areas where they can be left to grow and then easily dug in. The areas don't have to be large (perhaps raised beds or a few square metres) but working around existing crops is fiddly.

Pea family (leguminous) green manure crops help enrich the soil by taking ('fixing') nitrogen from the air to the root's nodules, so increasing nitrogen in the soil when they get dug back in.

Sowing

Green manures are usually sown in late summer or early autumn (when the soil's still warm enough for germination). Some are grown in summer, which will also suppress weeds and encourage beneficial insects. A small patch of crimson clover or *Phacelia tanacetifolia* will attract bees and hoverflies with their flowers which are invaluable at eating aphids. The easiest way is to broadcast sow them (sprinkling evenly across the soil surface) at the recommended rate. Rake the soil roughly level before sowing and then rake lightly onto the surface and water in.

You can also sow them in areas that you are planning on covering with light-excluding black plastic or landscape fabric (see the weeds section). Rather than

Green manure	type	comments
Buckwheat (*fagopyrum esculentum*)	Half-hardy annual	Fast growing. Takes up phosphates and disperses after digging in. Large leaves suppress weeds and flowers attract beneficial insects.
Red clover (*trifolium pratense*)	Hardy perennial	Lasts for two years or more, cut regular and use as a mulch. Good for larger-scale organic growing.
Fenugreek (*trigonella foenum-graecum*)	Half-hardy annual	Rapid boost to soil fertility in a few months. Plenty of foliage so good weed suppressor.
phacelia (*phacelia tanacetifolia*)	Half-hardy annual	Fast, strong-growing and spreading. Great weed suppressant. Blue flowers great for pollinators.
Mustard (*sinapis alba*)	Half-hardy annual	Very fast. Vigorous weed suppressant. Avoid dry.

dig in, place the plastic (or similar) over the plants and they'll break down into the soil as the weeds are killed off (double bubble!).

Digging in

They need digging in three or four weeks before sowing in that area, but you don't want the plants getting too woody either so time it by whichever comes first! You don't want them setting seed either (some do, and pretty fast) so if they look as if they will soon, get digging. Dig the plants into the top 25 cm of soil (no deeper, don't bury them) using a sharp spade that will chop them up at the same time.

Varieties – see chart:

sowing time	soil type	nitrogen fixer	how to sow	growing period
April-August	Good on poor soil	no	6 g per sq. m.	1-3 months
April-August	Most soils	yes	3 g per sq. m. shallow depth	2-18 months
March-August	Well drained	no	5 g per sq. m.	2-3 months
March-September	Most soils	no	16 g per sq. m.	1-3 months
March-September	Best on fertile soils	no	5 g per sq. m.	1-2 months

feeds

Feeding plants regularly gives them the nutrients they need to grow strongly and flower and fruit well. Most vegetables are hungry crops and produce higher yields if fed regularly.

what are they?

Fertilisers contain concentrated sources of plant nutrients (in chemical or organic form). I only use organic feeds, which is particularly important when growing edible plants. They tend to perform well, are more sustainable, environmentally friendly and over time help maintain the soil structure in a garden.

Fertilisers are based on the three major plant nutrients:

Nitrogen (N), for green leafy growth;

Phosphorus (P), for root and shoot growth; and

Potassium (K), for flowering and fruiting and general health and hardiness.

All proprietary fertilisers show their N:P:K ratio on the packaging, in that order. For example, a 20:20:20 indicates a balanced fertiliser for general growth, whereas a 10:12:24 has a high potassium fertiliser ratio, so is good for plants coming into flower and fruit.

Organic fertilisers contain plant nutrients in organic form and are derived from plant or animal sources. They tend to be slower acting than chemical feeds but are safer. Examples of organic fertilisers include: seaweed (a fine all-rounder, especially good for salads and fruit in containers); hoof and horn (leafy vegetables, plants); dried blood; fish blood and bone (excellent for base dressing trees and fruit bushes); chicken and poultry manure pellets (high in nitrogen so good for greening and leafy growth as well as flowers) and comfrey (great all-rounder, see the Comfrey section).

when to use

Feeds are usually applied in the growing seasons of spring and summer. Some (such as fish blood and bone or poultry manure pellets) are slow release so are applied in late winter or early spring for the growing season ahead.

Plants may also need feeding if they put on less growth than expected, produce lower yields of flowers or fruit or are showing signs of nutrient deficiency.

How to use

There are many ways to use them, and it all depends on what you're growing and where (in the ground, raised bed, in a pot etc.).

- **Watering in:** Liquid feeds are taken in and act quickly. They're great for plants grown in pots and containers, grow-bags, raised beds, etc. A regular weak feed tends to work best with moist plants and avoids root scorching. Water to the base for the roots to take in rather than splashing on the leaves.

- **Base dressing:** This is where you incorporate some feed into the soil or compost before planting. Pelleted chicken manure or fish blood and bone are ideal for general planting areas.

- **Foliar feeding:** This is a good technique if a plant looks sick through lack of nutrients and can quickly green them up again. Spray a weak solution (such as seaweed) onto the leaves and only when the plant is in shade to avoid scorching.

vegetables

vegetables

Artichokes (globe)

Great ornamental plants with silvery leaves. It's the flower buds that are eaten, delicious with vinaigrette or salted butter.

 Sow: March/April

 Harvest: August/September

 Site: Warm, sheltered sunny, with well-drained soil.

 Growing: Sow seed under cover in late winter or outdoors in early spring or buy ready-grown plants. Plant in mid-spring, spacing around 90 cm apart. Water during dry spells. Feed mid-spring and mulch generously. Cut down to ground level in autumn. Should get six to ten flower buds per plant.

 Varieties to try: Gros Vert de Laon (widely available and good flavour), Violetta di Chioggia (pretty purple variety to grow from seed).

 Tips: Allow plants to establish themselves properly before harvesting, which means snipping off buds when you see them in the first year to stop them flowering (painful but important!). Then, crop yearly. Replant every four or five years by growing on some of the offsets at the base in advance.

Artichokes (Jerusalem)

Delicious knobbly tubers that taste great in soups or baked, fried or roasted. Watch out for the after-effects (probably best to be out in the garden at this point!). Beautiful, sunflower-type flowers and very easy to grow as they come back year on year if you leave some in. Need room to spread though, so ideal allotment plant.

 Plant: February/March

 Harvest: January/February/March/October/ November/December

 Site: Not fussy about soil as long as it's not waterlogged or very acidic. As sunny as possible.

 Growing: Plant tubers 15 cm deep in late winter or early spring, spacing around 40 cm apart and 90 cm between rows.

 Varieties to try: Fuseau is very popular as it's less knobbly (so easier to peel!) and shorter at around 2 m. Many just plant from the greengrocer, so an unknown variety often works well.

 Tips: Bigger crops if you earth up when they're around 50 cm high. May need staking on a windy site and grow them where they won't shade out other crops as they can reach 3 m high! Leave them in the ground till you want them as they store best there.

delicious!

Asparagus

A delicious seasonal veg that comes up year on year once planted. Bit of a slow burner as plants need a few years to really produce but then they'll be good for many years to come.

 Plant: April

 Harvest: April/May/June

 Site: Needs a very well-drained spot in sun. Many grow them in designated raised bed.

 Growing: Plant 'crowns' (from specialist growers) in spring. Prepare the ground with plenty of organic matter, ideally the winter before planting. Dig a hole around 15 cm deep and build up a mound in the middle. Place the plant on the hole and spread the roots as evenly as possible down the mound and backfill with the crown slightly proud. Firm in and mulch over. Cut back ferny foliage in autumn.

 Varieties to try: 'Jersey Giant' (crops well over 2 weeks). 'Stewart's Purple' which is tasty, sweet and a beautiful purple too.

 Tips: This hurts but don't cut any spears for the first two summers after planting and then only take a few spears in year three. The idea is to build up the strength of the plant underground. After year three, harvest away (should get around 20–25 spears per plant) by cutting 15 cm spears (that's when they taste their best) to around 5 cm below ground level with a sharp knife and backfill the hole.

Aubergines

A popular vegetable that can be grown in the UK. Beautiful plants with purple flowers and shiny fruit.

 Sow: February/March

 Harvest: July/August/September

 Site: If you have a greenhouse or polytunnel, that's ideal but if not, best in pots in the sunniest, most protected spot in the garden. Can be grown in the ground in well-prepared, moisture-retentive soil.

 Growing: Sow seed indoors in early spring (germinate at around 21–24°C) and then prick out seedlings individually and grow on until early summer. Alternatively, buy ready-to-go plants (look for grafted ones that are vigorous and cope well with cooler weather) in early summer after frosts. Plant a couple to a large pot or space around 60 cm apart in the ground. Water regularly but don't drown and feed weekly once the fruits have set.

 Varieties to try: 'Moneymaker' has sausage-shaped fruit and is reliable and produces early so good for UK climate. 'Long purple' has been around for ages and produces lovely long dark shiny fruits.

 Tips: Pinch out top shoots when plants are 30 cm high to encourage side shoots. Support stems with canes to keep them nice and upright. Harvest when the fruit is nice and shiny and around 7.5 cm long or more and cut with around 1 cm of stem. Timing is key: if you leave them too long, they'll get bitter.

Beans (broad)

A firm favourite and very easy to grow and can be eaten fresh (tasting way better than anything you buy!) or stored. Many varieties to try.

 Sow: Sow in November or in March/April onwards for a good succession.

 Harvest: Late June for autumn-sown plants and then July/August/September.

 Site: The ideal soil is fertile, moisture-retentive and free-draining but most soils will produce a good crop as long as they're not waterlogged or too acidic. Ideally, prepare the soil the autumn before by adding plenty of well-rotted manure.

 Growing: Some sow into pots in late winter and early spring to get ahead of the game, but the easiest way is to sow in situ around mid-March. If you sow a few every couple of weeks, you'll get good succession. Space around 20 cm apart in rows, and with double rows, space around 80 cm apart if you have room so they cope better with the dry and can be hoed in-between. Water regularly when dry but feeding is not required.

 Varieties to try: 'Imperial Green Longpod' is tall and produces large yields of tasty bright green beans. 'The Sutton' is compact at around 30 cm tall and good for autumn sowing.

Tips: Support them well with posts (around 1.2 m above ground) and strings spaced at 30 cm intervals to hold rows upright. Can be eaten as young pods with immature beans within, shelled beans when mature or stored and dried.

Beans (French)

French beans are a must and extremely rewarding for first-time growers and ideal if you don't have much space. There are so many (purple, golden podded and heritage varieties) and the more you pick, the more they produce. They're simply divided into climbing (need support) and dwarf varieties (great for pots).

 Sow: April/May/June/July

 Harvest: June/July/August/September

 Site: The better the soil, the better the produce. Avoid waterlogged soils. Plenty of sun.

 Growing: They are frost tender, so sow indoors in pots or sow direct into the ground or pots in later spring. Wait till the soil's nice and warm, no rush! When sowing, sow two beans per hole and remove the weakest (or lift and move one) after germination. Space dwarf varieties around 15 cm apart and climbers around 20 cm. Grow climbers up wigwams, bamboo or hazel poles, on sunny wired fences, through trellis, etc. Feed occasionally.

 Varieties to try: 'Cobra' (climber) was my first and is prolific and has lovely lilac flowers. 'Purple Teepee' is a dwarf variety with, yup, you guessed it, dark purple pods that look great on the plate.

 Tips: Once they start producing, keep picking! Delicious young or mature but don't let them get fat or they get tough and the plant stops producing.

Beans (runner)

When I was a kid, I feared these tough, stringy things being served up. Growing and tasting them fresh off the plant, however, is a completely different ball game. Beautiful vigorous plants too and fabulous for pollinators.

 Sow: April/May (indoors), May/June (outdoors)

 Harvest: July/August/September/November

 Site: They require a sheltered sunny spot with fertile soil.

 Growing: Sow in pots indoors in mid-spring (to plant out in late spring) or sow direct in late spring around 25 cm apart. Never let them dry out, so water thoroughly and deeply in dry spells. They can be grown in large pots but feed and water regularly. Give them strong support (they get heavy) with wigwams or making up beanpole frames.

 Varieties to try: 'Scarlet Emperor' is many an allotmenteer's favourite. Early cropper with long straight beans. 'White Swan' has white flowers and produces long wide beans over a long period.

 Tips: Dig in plenty of compost or well-rotted manure the autumn before planting or even dig a pit (again in autumn) and fill it with shredded newspapers, organic matter, etc. so it composts down, and the beans can get their roots into it – nice and deep. Don't plant too many. Just a few plants will produce plenty.

Beetroot

OK, I'm a vegetable lover of course but, in truth, I've never liked beetroot! (Can't get past the muddy taste, although do try it every year in hope.) My family love it (roasted, boiled or the young leaves in a salad) and it's a good one to grow, so here goes.

 Sow: March/April/May/June. Early spring (bolt-resistant varieties) and others in mid-spring to mid-summer.

 Harvest: July to September

 Site: The top prizes are for those grown in deep sandy soils, but they do well in most soils if well prepared. Sunny spot.

 Growing: Prepare the soil in autumn, adding plenty of compost. Sow seed about 2.5 cm apart in rows and then thin them out to 7.5 cm for small ones or 15 cm if you want them to mature to full-sized roots. Water during dry spells and keep weed-free.

 Varieties to try: Burpees Golden with delicious yellow roots best picked small. 'Boltardy' is best for early sowing as doesn't run to seed easily and good taste too.

 Tips: Start 'pulling' them to thin them out as early as late spring and start eating. Best left in the ground till you want them and then lift any still left in mid-autumn.

Broccoli (sprouting)

Most of what we buy as broccoli with large green heads is actually calabrese (see Calabrese). Broccoli is a delicious winter vegetable with beautiful and tasty spears in hues of purple and white.

 Sow: April/May

 Plant out: June/July

 Harvest: January/February/March

 Site: Plenty of sun and a well-conditioned but firm soil. Can do well in containers and window boxes too ideally, without competition from other plants.

 Growing: Sow in spring direct into a well-prepared seedbed or plant out small plants in early- to mid-summer. They like very firm ground so don't be afraid to tread it over first. Feed in late summer and water in dry spells. They can be grown in large pots and containers spacing around 45 cm apart but you may need to make a cat's cradle affair with sticks and string over the top to keep pigeons off!

 Varieties to try: 'Early Purple Sprouting' is very popular for good reason as it's tough and reaches about 90 cm and ready about February/March. 'Late White Sprouting' extends the season into April and early May.

Tips: Once they start producing, start harvesting the spears to keep them ticking over, so check regularly, perhaps every few days (not every few hours!). Cut whole tender stems with a sharp knife, which will encourage them to produce more. If they start flowering, it's all over as the spears are woody and tasteless. One advantage is that they produce in winter when there are very few bugs around, so are usually pest-free.

Brussels sprouts

So, the vegetable that's divided the nation is now fashionable again (helps if you don't boil them to death!). Pretty easy to grow if you have some space and as with most, home-grown always tastes better, but it's what I'd call a slow burner.

 Sow: February/March/April

 Plant out: May/June

 Harvest: October to February

 Site: As with all Brassicas, a fertile firm soil is needed, so add plenty of organic matter. Sunny and sheltered.

 Growing: Plant out young plants in late spring after hardening off or in early summer, spacing around 60 cm apart. Firm in well and water during dry spells and feed in late summer.

 Varieties to try: F1 Hybrids are compact and produce uniform 'buttons'. 'Peer Gynt' is a favourite for good reason and peaks in November. 'Noisette' is a chef's favourite with a nutty flavour.

 Tips: Keep pigeons off young plants, which may mean netting them. Stake any that grow tall and look like they need it.

cabbages

Cabbages can be grown in a kaleidoscope of colours, textures and shapes. 'Summer and Autumn Hearting', 'Winter Hearting', 'Saveloy', and 'Spring Hearting' too. They need a book of their own but here's the basics:

 Sow: Spring Hearting in July/August and the others around April/May.

 Harvest: Well, all year round if you grow them all!

 Site: Sunny spot. Prepare well in autumn for spring planting.

 Growing: As with all brassicas, firm in very well, water during dry spells (don't let them dry out) and space around 30 to 45 cm apart depending on variety, the more room the better. Apply high nitrogen feed in summer for plenty of leafy growth to build up a nice plant.

 Varieties to try: Too many! One for each season: 'Golden Acre' is summer hearting, 'Hispi' is a fine summer-into-autumn choice with small hearts. 'January King' is a lovely crisp Saveloy. 'Wheelers Imperial' is spring hearting.

 Tips: Leave them on their stems till you want to eat them. The dreaded 'Clubroot' can be a big problem with all brassicas, especially cabbages. The roots swell and rot, so the top becomes stunted. Once it's there, it can stay in the ground for 20 years. It's less prevalent on chalky, alkaline soils and is best avoided by raising your own plants from seed.

calabrese

Yes, the one commonly known as 'green broccoli'. Large solid heads (very good for you). If you're limited with space, go for broccoli but if you have a big garden or allotment, then grow some of these as well.

 Sow: March/April/May

 Harvest: June–September

 Site: Yes, as with all brassicas (you're getting the hang of it now, eh?) a nice fertile well-compacted soil on the neutral to alkaline side. Plenty of sun.

 Growing: Sow undercover in spring or into an outdoor seedbed in mid spring and then plant outdoors in late spring. Space around 30 cm apart. Keep weed-free.

 Varieties to try: 'Romanesco' is a late cropper with a soft texture and should be steamed. 'Shogun' has large blue-green heads with many smaller offshoots beneath and is an early cropper.

 Tips: If you crop the head and leave the plant in the ground, you'll get some smaller spears a few weeks later – double bubble! The trick with all brassicas is to keep them growing steadily (they don't like surprises), so stable moisture conditions and an occasional feed.

And they supposedly help you see in the dark!

carrots

One of the only vegetables I ate as a young child (along with baked beans!). Pulling a homegrown-carrot is very exciting as you're never quite sure what it'll come out like.

 Sow: April/May/June

 Harvest: July–October

 Site: They are fussy about soil. Ideally deep, fertile and sandy. Dig over and remove as many stones as possible or they'll bend around them. If you have stony soil, grow short, rounded varieties. Some are ideal for growing in deep containers; those that 'grow to show' grow them in dustbins!

 Growing: They have to be planted in situ as they don't transplant. Sow as thinly as possible in shallow drills in the ground in rows 30 cm apart in early spring and use fleece to keep frosts off. When growing in containers, you can broadcast sow and then thin them out later. Keep weed-free and water well in dry spells, encouraging them to prospect down.

 Varieties to try: 'Early Nantes' has great flavour and colour, 'Chantenay Red Cored' is medium-sized, smooth-skinned and 'Parmex' is good in poor soil.

 Tips: Sow thinly but they'll need thinning out (to about 8 cm gaps), which attracts the dreaded carrot fly. Those in containers will hopefully combat these flies as they can only fly very low! Pull some young and let others mature.

cauliflower

One of those vegetables that get a bad rep because of millions of them being boiled to death. There are now many colours and varieties to choose from for year-round caulis and, come on, you simply can't beat a good home-grown cauliflower cheese! Not the easiest veg to grow but if you have the right conditions, give them a try.

 Sow: Summer heading in January/February to plant out in March/April, harvest May to July; autumn heading in March to plant out April/May, harvest August to October; and winter heading in April/May to plant out in May/June, harvest February to April.

 Site: Well-consolidated fertile soil on the alkaline side ideally (like all brassicas). If digging over, leave a few months between digging and planting. Sunny spot.

 Growing: Sow summer varieties indoors, autumn varieties indoors to start off, or a seedbed outdoors and winter varieties in a seedbed outdoors. Once they're established as decent plants, give them a high nitrogen feed around mid-summer. Water regularly and keep weed-free.

 Varieties to try: 'All The Year Round', a fine starter that works across the year, 'Romanesco' is a beautiful looking one with lime-green curds (that's the flower-shaped head bit!) and 'Purple Cape' has beautiful purple curds in winter.

Tips: As the head develops, bend some of the outer leaves over it to keep good colour (especially with white ones as they can go brown – not very appealing!). When growing a few, cut some young as they'll be very tasty and will avoid a glut later on.

celeriac

This is not going to win any beauty parades and certainly can't be called an 'ornamental edible', but it is becoming very popular and much easier to grow than celery. It's sometimes called 'turnip-rooted celery' so, you guessed it, it's a root crop. Versatile, so good in soups, as a cooked winter vegetable (baked, mashed) or grated raw in salads.

 Sow: March

 Harvest: January–March and September–October

 Site: Likes a fertile soil, as good as you can give it, so dig in plenty of well-rotted manure or compost. Likes sun but can cope with a little shade.

 Growing: Sow early indoors (on a windowsill is good), then prick out into individual pots and grow on before hardening off and planting out after the last frost. Space around 30 to 40 cm apart. Feed every two weeks with a liquid feed. Remove side shoots from mid-summer onwards to form a nice upright plant and in late summer draw soil up over any exposed root.

 Varieties to try: 'Ibis' is fast growing and smooth-skinned, 'Prinz' has a fine flavour.

 Tips: Harvest from October on. The flavour doesn't deteriorate with age or size so dig when you want them unless your soil is wet and claggy, in which case lift and store them by the end of November as they may rot off. Cut the tops and side shoots off with a sharp knife before eating or storing.

chillies

Who loves a spicy kick? I do. There's a huge range of chillies to grow, from mild to very hot and in a kaleidoscope of colours. They do particularly well on a sunny windowsill (you don't even need a garden) and some do well outdoors on a sun-baked patio. Start them off from seed or buy small plants and watch them grow and fruit.

 Sow: February/March

 Harvest: July–October

 Site: Sheltered and sunny, they hate cold snaps and wind.

 Growing: Sow in seed trays indoors (they germinate at around 21–24°C) and when seedlings are big enough to handle, prick out into individual 3-cm pots and then pot them up into larger pots when the roots fill the pot nicely. If placing outside, wait till the last frost is over as they're tender. Water regularly and reduce if conditions cool and feed weekly with a tomato feed.

 Varieties to try: 'Joe's Long Cayenne' (nothing to do with me but a great cropper with 30-cm slim chillies), 'Apache' is mid-strength and compact so great for windowsills or window boxes and for a hot one, how about 'Naga Viper', at 1.349 million on the Scoville Heat Unit or SHU for short (a measure of spiciness), this is one of the very hottest.

Tips: Keep picking and they'll keep producing. They can be harvested young when green (maybe take some) or left to mature and ripen. Either use straight away or dry them and store in dry jars. Snip off the whole chilli with a little of the green stalk. When things cool in late summer, bring outdoor plants inside to prolong fruiting.

courgettes and marrows

OK, so I've put these together as a marrow is often a courgette that's been forgotten to be picked! They are delicious and far tastier than shop-bought. One or two plants will do it as once they get going, they produce plenty and you'll be looking at every courgette recipe in the book. Great in the ground or in large pots/half barrels.

 Sow: April, plant out May/June

 Harvest: June–October

 Site: They love a rich fertile soil with plenty of compost or well-rotted manure or use a peat-free multipurpose compost if growing in pots.

 Growing: Sow the flat seed into small pots on their side (it stops them rotting off), two to a pot and place on a windowsill or similar. Remove the weakest once they show. Grow them on and plant outdoors after the last frost into the ground or a large container, stand back and watch them grow! Water regularly, keeping the soil always just moist and feed every two weeks. They'll need plenty of room, around 1 m² in the ground per plant or a large pot or growbag each.

 Varieties to try: 'Clarion' is pale green with a good flavour cooked or raw, 'Parador' has lovely yellow fruits all summer, 'Tiger Cross' is stripy, fruits early and stores well (and turns into a marrow for stuffing!).

Tips: If they fail to produce fruit, it's almost always down to cold weather or being too dry. You can hand pollinate the female flowers too using a dry paintbrush between the flowers. Once they start producing, start picking. Cut them when they're small (around 10 cm) which encourages the plant to produce more.

Look at those gorgeous colours!

cucumber

Yes, cucumbers can be grown in the UK and as with most home-grown edibles, are very tasty and in this case super crunchy too. As you can imagine, they are tender plants that require regular attention and support (I mean to grow them up but talking to them helps too of course!). They can be grown in a greenhouse if you have one but if you have a protected sunny garden, try them outdoors.

 Sow: April, plant May

 Harvest: July–October

 Site: A warm sheltered spot.

 Growing: Sow seed one to a pot on their side in mid-spring for indoor growing and late spring for outdoor. One or two plants will do it. Transfer indoor plants into larger (10 cm) pots around late May in an unheated greenhouse (or use a growbag and one of those mini greenhouses?).

 Support: With indoor cucumbers, grow them up a bamboo cane, tying it in gently as it heads skywards. Outdoor plants are best grown up a simple wigwam or netting (on a sunny fence or wall?). Okay – tricky bit alert! For decent-sized cukes, they need pruning by removing all side shoots from the bottom 60 cm, which encourages higher side shoots to develop. Feed every two weeks. When they get to around 20 cm long, they should have a tiny cucumber complete with a flower at the tip. Snip off the end of the shoot a couple of leaves past the fruit. Keep nipping out tips to encourage these chosen fruits to get bigger; if you don't, no biggie, you'll end up with lots of smaller ones. They grow fast so keep tying into their supports. Watering is the key. Don't overwater when young as it can make them rot off, but when they are near to cropping, water well, steadily building it up to the crescendo!

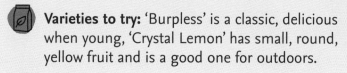 **Varieties to try:** 'Burpless' is a classic, delicious when young, 'Crystal Lemon' has small, round, yellow fruit and is a good one for outdoors.

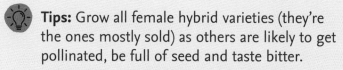 **Tips:** Grow all female hybrid varieties (they're the ones mostly sold) as others are likely to get pollinated, be full of seed and taste bitter.

Fennel (Florence)

Beautiful and delicious. Grown for its swollen aniseed-flavoured bulbs, which are delicious. Crunchy in salads and fabulous when roasted in amongst other vegetables. Its feathery foliage is a fine garnish. Downsides are it's notoriously fussy and tricky to grow as it's dependant on a warm steady summer. Did I mention I won first prize at my allotment? Pure luck, perfect weather!

 Sow: Under cover April, outdoors in May

 Harvest: August/September

 Site: Sunny, well-drained soil. Ideally add some humus (like leaf mould) the winter before.

 Growing: Start off indoors, three seeds to a small pot and take out the two weakest once germinated. Harden off before planting out and the key is to be patient until there is steady warm weather, they hate fluctuations. Space around 25 cm apart. Water when dry and earth up a little until the bulb is golf ball sized.

 Varieties to try: 'Goal' has large full-flavoured bulbs, 'Fennel di Firenze' is fast growing and mild.

 Tips: The weather is out of one's hands (needs a long, warm and steady summer). Water at first, don't let them dry out but don't drown. Steady watering as the bulb develops. Any stress such as dryness, fluctuation in temperature, not enough organic matter, not praising them enough, etc., makes the bolt inedible!

Garlic

Surprisingly tough, easy to grow and fresh garlic is juicy, delicious and very good for you of course.

 Sow: November or February/March

 Harvest: June, July, August

 Site: Full sun, a fertile rich soil that keeps moisture around the roots.

 Growing: Plant whole (firm and large, discard tiny or soft ones) cloves ideally in late autumn, which means roots are formed ready to put on plenty of growth come spring and so make earlier to harvest, larger bulbs. Plant with the tip a couple of cm below the surface. It really is a case of plant a clove and produce a bulb. Space around 15 cm apart. Try to keep some moisture in the ground at all times. Can be grown in pots. Harvest 'wet' as and when you need them by pulling, and the rest harvest around mid-summer (autumn planted) or late summer (spring planted) when the foliage dies off.

 Varieties to try: 'Purple Wight' doesn't store too well but is best eaten fresh, 'Provence Wight' is sweet tasting.

 Tips: Avoid supermarket bulbs (may be for specific climates) and always plant disease-free certified bulbs produced specifically for growing. Leave on the ground for a few days in the sun to dry off. Birds tend to peck at the emerging growth come spring so replant/cover with twigs till established.

kale

An easy brassica to grow (unlike some!) and great for producing healthy fresh veg throughout the winter when there's little else around. Delicious steamed or in a stir-fry.

 Sow: April, May, June

 Harvest: December to April

 Site: Nice rich firm soil – neutral to alkaline.

 Growing: Sow in small pots of seed trays, harden off and plant out from May onwards. Space around 45 cm.

 Varieties to try: 'Black Tuscany' with tasty strappy black/green leaves, 'Dwarf Green Curled' is tasty, good for poor soils and windy sites.

 Tips: Take a few leaves when young (just some, don't be greedy, so the plant keeps growing) in early winter and, once matured, pick as you need.

Kohlrabi

This is a delicious root vegetable (like a mild turnip, delicious in soups) that can be tricky to find in shops. It's quite easy to grow as long as you keep an eye on it; occasional singing helps.

 Sow: April/May/June

 Harvest: July/August/September

 Site: Alkaline fertile, well-compacted soil in sun.

 Growing: Best sown in situ from mid-spring onwards. Thin to about 15 cm apart. Regular watering is essential to keep them ticking over and steadily growing without dry periods.

 Varieties to try: 'Blusta' produces purple bulbs with crisp, white flesh and 'Kolibri' is another with purple skin and a bitter-free taste.

 Tips: Start eating them young (around golf ball size) and try to get through them all (freeze or they last for around two weeks in the fridge) before they get too big as they get too fibrous inside.

Leeks

I was brought up on leeks in cheese sauce!! I love growing them too, especially harvesting some as baby leeks. They're easy and hardy. If you have enough space (an allotment ideally), grow a few different ones, which will give you some leeks in most months of the year.

 Sow: March/April

 Harvest: January–March and September–December

 Site: Fertile (even heavy but not waterlogged) soil and plenty of moisture, think Welsh conditions.

 Growing: Sow direct in drills or start off in a seedbed and then carefully transplant when they're around 15 cm tall. Rather than firming the soil around them, 'dib' a hole around 15 cm deep, place the small plant in and water in with a watering can to settle the roots – job done. Space around 15 cm apart in rows 30 cm apart.

 Varieties to try: 'Musselburgh' has thick stems and is very hardy and 'Bandit' is very tasty.

 Tips: The smaller the tastier, so don't leave to grow big. Lift gently with a fork rather than forcing them out. A good tip is not to shake the soil off there and then as it can get stuck in the leaves of other leeks and will then be very tricky to get out. They are a little prone to bolting if there are large fluctuations in temperature or moisture. I've found sowing outdoors rather than trying to start them off early under cover gives best results.

Lettuce and salad leaves (cut-and-come-again)

There's a whole world of lettuce and leaves out there. The easiest way (and it's almost like mustard and cress) is to grow them as a 'cut-and-come-again' crop; you know, the ones you buy limp in mixed bags at the supermarket. They're very easy, can be grown in beds, raised beds, growbags or large pots.

 Sow: May to August

 Harvest: June to October

 Site: Sunny, well drained. Peat-free multipurpose is fine for containers.

 Growing: The best way is to 'broadcast sow' a patch. Water the soil first (to stop the small seed being displaced) then sow thinly and sieve a little compost over the top. Water regularly using a fine rose on a watering can and feed every two weeks with a weak organic liquid feed.

 Varieties to try: There are so many that can be grown this way, including Chinese mustard greens, pak choi, rocket, lamb's lettuce, mizuna, etc. Either grow individually or buy pre-mixed combos (like Mediterranean mixes or Oriental mixes) or try mixing your own as an experiment. Some are ready for their first harvest in as little as 20 days.

Tips: Once the leaves get to around 10 cm long, start harvesting. A pair of kitchen scissors is best. Cut almost to ground level and then water and feed and they'll reshoot a few times. One of two varieties may grow larger than others so either pull them out or snip back and eat.

Onions

Onions are of course one of the most used vegetables in the kitchen and sure, they're not expensive in the shops but are a very satisfying crop to grow your own and means you can try some different varieties out, and really know your onions! The larger ones are 'slow burners', taking around 15 weeks to mature so, if you only have limited space, maybe this is one to miss out and go for spring onions instead.

 Sow: Seed under cover December to February or buy 'sets' (baby onions) and plant out from September to November or in March. Spring onions can be sown outside anytime between March and August.

 Harvest: June to September

 Site: Good drainage and sun essential.

 Growing: The easiest way is to buy sets in autumn (for overwintering onions) or early spring (for maincrop onions) and plant directly outdoors. Space around 10 cm apart in rows 20 cm apart. Keep them watered as fluctuations between dry and wet may encourage bolting. Sow spring onions every few weeks from spring to midsummer to get a good succession going and thin out to around 2.5 cm apart (and eat the thinnings, which are a little like chives).

 Varieties to try: 'Red Baron' is a fine red onion with great flavour, 'White Lisbon' produces small white golf-ball sized onions with silver skin.

Tips: Weed regularly around them and check your hoe fits between the rows nicely before planting to make life easier. Harvest maincrops once the leaves turn yellow and die back, lift, and leave in the sun to dry off for a few days. Those grown over winter can be lifted and used when they look big enough (or when you need them) and just pulled as and when.

parsnips

Parsnips are a fabulous autumnal and winter veg and very hardy so can be left in the ground over winter and harvested when needed. Shop-bought ones can be underwhelming so if you have space and time, give them a go to taste the difference. You really do need patience with traditional varieties, they can be tricky to germinate and take 9 months to grow to maturity (but it's even more rewarding when they come good). Baby varieties take up less space and mature more quickly.

 Sow: Outside April–May

 Harvest: November–February

 Site: Well drained and sandy and sunny.

 Growing: Sow in situ, thinly, around 2.5 cm apart. The seeds are quite large and easy to handle. Thin to around 15 cm once they get going. Water in dry spells deep down to encourage the roots to prospect downwards and weed around them.

 Varieties to try: 'Gladiator' is relatively quick to mature, 'Javelin' is very tasty or 'Dagger' is a great baby variety with smooth roots.

 Tips: Use fresh seed every year. Wait until a frost has hit them in the ground, which really sweetens them up and makes all the difference to their taste. Leave them in the ground unless it gets very wet, in which case lift and store. With baby varieties, only use specific seed as traditional varieties can't be eaten early.

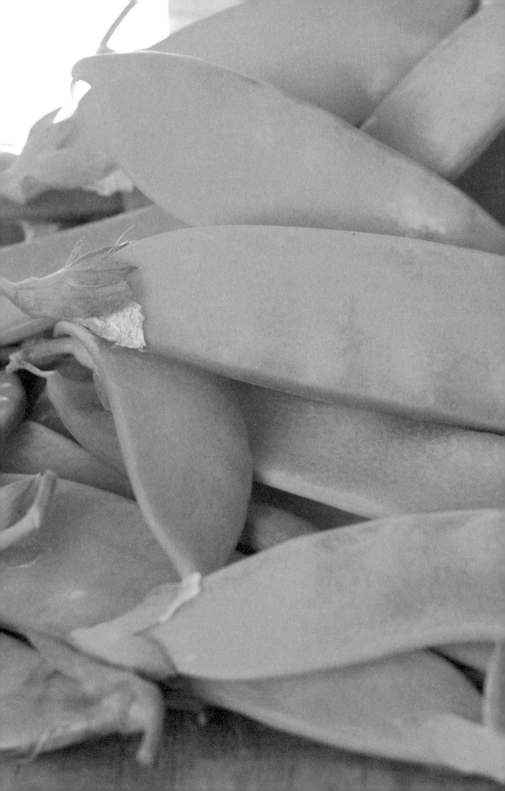

Mangetout and sugar snap

The truth is, growing 'proper' peas in a pod is not all that easy. They require regular care and can often get munched along the way (by mice as seed or maggots in the pod) and require regular harvesting. Mangetout and sugar snap are far easier, home-grown are delectable and they can be eaten at various stages.

 Sow: Mangetout and sugar snap: April–June direct or earlier under cover

 Harvest: June–September

 Site: Open, sunny site with good drainage.

 Growing: Sow early under cover (in polytunnels or in pots to plant out after frosts) or sow direct, staggered in rows in flat-bottomed drills spacing around 7.5 cm apart in all directions. Provide some support for them to scramble through such as pea sticks (twigs about 1.2 m tall pushed into the ground) or with some simple posts and wire netting. Keep well watered in dry weather, feed occasionally and never let them dry out!

 Varieties to try: 'Golden Sweet' is a tall, pretty and delicious mangetout and 'Oregon Sugar Pod' has a long cropping season.

 Tips: Once they start producing, keep picking to encourage more and stop them going over. Pick mangetout young at about 5 cm long, sugar snap at about 4 cm. Discard those that have gone stringy. Sugar snap can be left to develop in the pod a little and 'shelled'.

peppers

Home-grown peppers are fun and although they may not reach the size of shop-bought ones, their sweet tender flesh is very tasty. They can be grown indoors (you'll have more chance of colouring up the red ones) or placed in a pot or a couple in a growbag or planted into the ground outdoors in a protected sunny spot. Grow from seed or buy plants ready to go.

 Sow: February/March, plant out May/June

 Harvest: June–September

 Site: As sunny and hot as possible. Well-drained fertile soil.

 Growing: Sow seed on a windowsill or in a heated propagator and then prick out the seedlings into individual pots and grow them on indoors, aiming for a temperature between 16 and 20°C. Pot on again and place in a greenhouse, or polytunnel if you have one, for best results or harden off and take or plant outdoors. They can be planted out. Feed weekly with a tomato feed and keep tying them in to a support like a bamboo cane.

 Varieties to try: 'Bell Boy' produces well, it starts green and may ripen to red, 'Sweet Chocolate' has dark purple skin and is good in tricky climates (like ours!).

 Tips: Don't wait for them all to turn red, start cropping and eating and if some do it's a bonus.

potatoes

There is a whole world of potatoes out there just waiting to be grown, boiled, roasted and mashed! Maincrops require space and are slow burners so I'm focussing on the small, waxy pink or purpled-skinned 'salad' or 'new' potatoes that taste noticeably different dug fresh. Depending on which varieties you choose (first earlies or second earlies, sounds complicated but really isn't) they'll take between 10 and 14 weeks to harvest. If you choose a few of each and plant them at the same time, it should mean that you stagger the harvest nicely.

 Sow: 'Seed potatoes' late March/April

 Harvest: July onwards

 Site: Potatoes like deep well-drained moisture-retentive soil and sun. Add plenty of compost when planting. They also do well in large pots or pop-up potato bags using regular peat-free potting compost.

 Growing: Not essential, but research says chitting salad seed potatoes improves cropping. Chitting means leaving them in a cool, dry, light place until some shoots develop. Start around February/March. Old egg boxes are ideal for holding them in. Plant to a depth of around 30 cm in the ground in trenches and 20 cm in pots. Plant approximately four seed potatoes in a dustbin-sized planter or adjust depending on container. Once foliage shows above ground, protect it from any late frosts by keeping some fleece handy to cover them over. 'Earthing up' is when you pull the soil from either side of the rows to cover the new stems. This protects the plants from late frosts and increases yield. In containers, simply add more compost to bring the levels up.

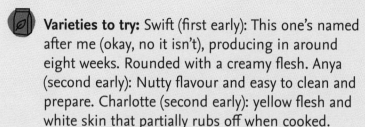 **Varieties to try:** Swift (first early): This one's named after me (okay, no it isn't), producing in around eight weeks. Rounded with a creamy flesh. Anya (second early): Nutty flavour and easy to clean and prepare. Charlotte (second early): yellow flesh and white skin that partially rubs off when cooked.

Tips: Hungry plants, so feeding and watering are essential. A liquid feed, general fertiliser or specific potato feed will work. Apply a high potash fertiliser every couple of weeks. Water regularly, try not to let the soil dry out and for better crops, look to maintain a constant soil moisture throughout the growing season. When the plant's flowers open and the foliage is still green, they're ready to harvest. You can have a gentle dig around the potato tubers to lift a few little'uns especially early or have a sneaky look to check they're ready.

Radish

Radish are very easy to grow and fast too, ready to eat in about eight weeks. They're usually seen as part of a salad, but they can be used in stir-fries, pickled, thrown into risottos. They're ideal as a filler crop that can be grown between others and sown throughout spring and summer.

 Sow: March–August

 Harvest: May–September

 Site: Fertile soil that doesn't dry out and partial shade helps stop them running to seed.

 Growing: Sow in situ in shallow drills and then thin to around 2.5 cm between seedlings (you can eat the thinnings). Keep well watered and weed free ... that's about it. Told you they were easy!

 Varieties to try: 'Scarlet Globe' is crispy and hot, 'French Breakfast' is a classic, very popular and good cropper.

 Tips: Best eaten fresh from the ground if possible and better young than old as they go all woody. Sow a few every couple of weeks to avoid gluts and keep them going all summer long.

shallots

With onions, you plant one set and get one onion, but with shallots, you plant one and get shallots of them! Boom boom. They are viewed as 'gourmet onions' and chefs get rather snooty about cooking with them rather than onions as they are milder and sweeter, and provide the ideal raw crunch in salads and dressings, but when finely chopped and fried, break down to create a smooth texture for a range of sauces.

 Sow: Plant sets February/March

 Harvest: July/August

 Site: Good drainage and plenty of sun is essential.

 Growing: Dig in plenty of compost to enrich the soil and then rake level. Plant the sets (which are single small shallots) approximately 20 cm apart as they do grow into a sizeable clump. Simply push the set into the ground so it's half in, half out. Water in prolonged dry spells and feed occasionally with a general liquid fertiliser. Try to avoid overhead watering, as this can encourage fungal diseases.

 Varieties to try: 'Golden Gourmet' is a rounded shallot with a light golden skin and prolific cropper with approximately 8–10 shallots from each plant. 'Jermor' is juicy and a classic 'longue' French shape.

 Tips: After planting, cover with twigs or fleece to stop birds digging them up. Stop watering and feeding once shallot bulbs have swollen in mid-summer. Watering spring-planted crops after mid-summer can mean they don't store so well.

Spinach

One of the easiest vegetables to grow and can be eaten in all stages of growth; pick the leaves young within a month of sowing and have them in salads or let them mature for steaming or stir-frying. If you sow in summer and autumn, you can have it available all year round too. And we all know how good it is for us, right?

 Sow: Summer spinach March–May; autumn spinach August–October

 Harvest: Summer May–September; autumn September–November

 Site: Spinach grows in all soils except for poor dry soil and does best in partial shade.

 Growing: Check packet first as most, but not all, varieties are for autumn sowing. Sow thinly in rows in situ or broadcast a few seeds around a large pot or in a raised bed. Water regularly and feed occasionally. They dislike hot and dry, which encourages them to bolt, especially if summer sown.

 Varieties to try: 'Medania' is a good all-year-rounder and great for baby leaves, 'Picasso' has a fine texture.

Tips: To keep a good harvest of young leaves, sow every month during the growing season. Grow them as a 'cut-and-come-again' crop by snipping them off and they'll regrow. 'Perpetual spinach' isn't quite the same, the leaves are shiny and tougher so have a different texture but still taste good. They grow all year round and can cope with hot summers and keep going into the winter too so may be worth growing some too.

squashes

Squashes are great fun and celebrate autumn beautifully but do need some serious room to grow so you'll need plenty of space as plants will spread between 3 m and 5 m in diameter. Pumpkins need even more so I'll leave those to the allotmenteers and competition growers! Squashes are more versatile and tastier anyway, great roasted, in soups or added to seasonal stews.

 Sow: April

 Harvest: October

 Site: The more soil preparation, the better. Plenty of manure and ideally a fertile, moisture-retentive soil. Some dig a hole the autumn before and chuck any organic matter in there (as well as shredded paper and cardboard) so a plant can get its roots down into it. They're sometimes grown on compost heaps too where there's more space.

 Growing: Sow seed individually in pots on windowsills, grow on and then harden off before planting out after the last frost. Make a ring of soil around the plant (about 30 cm diameter) and water into it each time and stand back as they take off! Feed and water religiously and then ease off in late summer to encourage ripening and snip off a few leaves so the sun can get to the fruit.

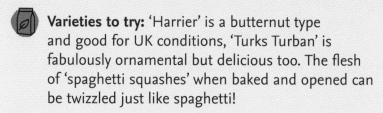 **Varieties to try:** 'Harrier' is a butternut type and good for UK conditions, 'Turks Turban' is fabulously ornamental but delicious too. The flesh of 'spaghetti squashes' when baked and opened can be twizzled just like spaghetti!

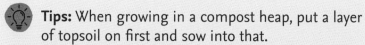 **Tips:** When growing in a compost heap, put a layer of topsoil on first and sow into that.

sweetcorn

I can still remember the first time I tasted my home-grown sweetcorn, having picked it and chucked it into some boiling water there and then on my allotment. The taste was unbelievable, so sweet and juicy – the best I'd ever tasted. I'd say it's the one vegetable with the biggest difference in taste to shop-bought. You'll only get a couple of cobs per plant on average.

 Sow: April indoors, plant out May/June

 Harvest: July–September

 Site: Sheltered, sunny with good fertile soil

 Growing: Sow one to a pot on a windowsill or heated propagator in spring. Grow on in a cool sunny spot and then harden off and plant out. Space around 45 cm apart and keep some fleece handy for colder nights so they establish quickly. Water in dry spells and mulch roots with organic matter.

 Varieties to try: 'Moonshine' has won some tasting trials recently. 'Swift' (no relation) is fast-maturing and delicious. 'Minipop' produces baby cobs (plant 20 cm apart and pick before pollination before the tassels turn brown).

 Tips: Plant them in blocks, not rows as they are wind-pollinated so it ensures good pollination. They're ready when their tassels turn brown and dry up. Check by peeling back some green sheath and squeeze a kernel. If the juice is clear, wait a few more days but watch out for the birds who are waiting too and if the juice is milky, get that water boiling!

Swiss chard

Some varieties have such pretty leaves that some people grow it in their garden for its ornamental value. It's easy to grow and tough as old boots (not to eat!). It holds its body when cooked too, either steamed, stir-fried or boiled.

 Sow: April–July

 Harvest: July to October

 Site: Grows on most soils but the more muck and moisture you can give it, the better.

 Growing: Sow direct from mid spring onwards 15 cm apart in rows around 30 cm apart. Or plant in containers or pop directly in flower beds. Water in dry spells and water regularly and that's about it.

 Varieties to try: 'Bright Lights' has red, white and yellow leaves and 'Fordhook Giant' has thick white stems and dark green leaves, which might make it not as pretty as others but is probably the best tasting.

 Tips: Crop individual leaves with a sharp knife. Start cropping as soon as they look big enough to use and they'll keep coming. With larger leaves, look out for snails before cooking!

Tomatoes

Tomatoes really warrant a book of their own, but I'll try and keep things simple. There are so many different varieties such as Beefsteak, Yellow, Striped, Cherry, Plum, Roma, Heirloom, etc. Here's some info on how to grow them outdoors. My thinking is that if you have a greenhouse, you'll probably know quite a bit already! They do need regular love and attention but in a good summer are so worth it.

 Sow: March, plant outdoors May/June

 Harvest: July–October

 Site: Sunny, warm and sheltered with plenty of compost added. Good in the ground if well drained or grow in raised beds, pots or growbags.

 Growing: For a few plants, sow seed into pots and for loads, sow into seed trays and place on the windowsill. Don't sow too early or you'll end up with leggy plants. Plant outdoors into their final spot after the last frosts, spacing around 75 cm apart (depending on variety). Support them with stakes or supports and tie in, water and feed (liquid tomato feed) regularly, even a weak feed with every watering. When side shoots appear where the leaf stalk joins the stem, pinch them out when they're about 2.5 cm long. When plants reach around 1.2 m, remove lower leaves below the first truss (set of fruit) and keep removing any yellowing leaves to allow light and air to circulate. In late summer, pick off any flowers that will never have time to fruit.

Varieties to try: 'Gardeners Delight' is a huge favourite with small, tasty fruit, 'Outdoor Girl' is a classic in shape and taste and in colder areas try 'Glacier', which is more forgiving, but still tasty of course.

Tips: For first-timers, rather than growing from seed maybe buy some young plants like 'Tumbler' and pop them into containers and pots and place somewhere sunny (they trail and don't need support). The most common problem with tomatoes is inconsistent watering, which leads to skin cracking and 'blossom end rot' – sounds painful, doesn't it!

perennial vegetables

Almost all the vegetables we grow are annuals but there are some we can plant into our gardens, harvest and they'll come back year on year. They work well within an ornamental garden set-up and purveyors of permaculture swear by them. I haven't grown all of them myself, there's plenty out there – here's a few to try out.

Earthnut Pea (Lathyrus tuberosus)

Ancient hardy perennial vegetable. Is leguminous and nitrogen fixing too (a good thing!) and grown for 'tuberous peas' that can be roasted or boiled and have a delicious nutty taste. The foliage is pretty and the flowers are pink and sweet scented. Given support, it will climb or can be left to trail.

Skirret (Sium sisarum)

Top European veg before potatoes were introduced and took over! A hardy perennial root vegetable with a flavour somewhere between a carrot and parsnip and attractive flowers that are great for pollinators. Save seed each year or grow from small plants growing at the base.

welsh onion (Allium fistulosum)

Comes from Asia, not Wales! It's a fully hardy and very useful perennial onion that can be harvested most months of the year except deepest winter. It doesn't form bulbs, it's the leaves that taste like spring onions that are eaten.

Buckler-leaved sorrel (Rumex scutatus)

Incredibly easy to grow as a leafy groundcover in the garden. Its leaves have a fresh, tangy, lemony flavour that works well in salads when young or, when more mature, cook them like spinach.

Sea kale (Crambe maritima)

A fine leafy garden plant that can cope with coastal conditions. The tender shoots are eaten like asparagus, the leaves used like spinach or regular garden kale, the younger the better as they can turn bitter when old (like us all).

mashua or perennial nasturtium (Tropaeolum tuberosum)

A vigorous climber so you'll need space to let it do its thing. Its edible tubers (it produces masses so save some for replanting) taste like a crunchy, slightly smoked radish when raw and, when cooked, turn soft with a fennel flavour. They're pretty too, with orange trumpet flowers.

yacón (Smallanthus sonchifolius)

Grown for its large edible roots. They have a sweet, crisp, refreshing taste, hard to describe, but imagine a mix of apple, pear and celery! Lift and leave in sunlight for a few days to sweeten up. Bought in small rhizomes, easy to grow and can be grown as a perennial crop or lifted and replanted each year.

herbs

Fresh herbs are undeniably more delicious than the dried, papery packet ones. Growing them is supremely satisfying and picking and using fresh herbs straight from the garden is what it's all about. We'd all love a designated herb garden, even 'potager' perhaps but most of us simply don't have the space. Fortunately, many herbs can be slotted into an existing garden, grown between ornamentals, and in containers or raised beds. I have a few random pots that give a corner of my garden that shabby chic (or is it 'upcycled'!) look and they do really well, enjoying the free-draining conditions a pot offers.

Some, such as bay, rosemary, thyme and sage are hardy, woody and evergreen, whereas perennial herbs such as mint and chives die back and come back year on year. Annual herbs are non-hardy; they are one-year wonders, programmed to grow, flower and seed in one season. They require more care overall and will need sowing from seed or buying in small pots to grow on each year (although some such as French tarragon can come back if overwintered in a frost-free area such as a greenhouse or cold frame). A good cheat is to buy those supermarket herbs in spring and plant them into pots outdoors after the last frosts in spring or grow on your windowsill, as they usually do pretty well there.

A range of herbs across the board is ideal; grow what you like best. The one thing most herbs do need is plenty of sun. There are a few, such as mint, parsley, lemon balm, coriander, chervil (if spring-sown) and golden oregano that will grow in partial shade but if you want to build up a good range, then look to your garden's sunniest spot to grow them in. The sun will not only help them grow vigorously, so there is plenty of tasty young growth to harvest but also brings the essential oils to the plant's surface to maximise their flavour.

Growing in containers

All herbs enjoy an easy root run. Multipurpose peat-based compost is too light and has the tendency to dry out. A loam-based compost such as John Innes No. 1 with around 25% added grit or perlite is an ideal medium. Keep the soil moist but not wet (watering in the morning is best), watering when the top of the soil has dried out and use a general organic feed such as liquid seaweed to encourage foliage growth.

shrubby herbs

Bay – Vigorous evergreen shrubs that can be shaped to form topiary pieces or left to grow loose. They look good in a pot as a focal point and one plant is usually more than enough for the kitchen. If grown in pots, use a John Innes No. 3 compost and wrap it in cold winters. Avoid windy spots.

Sage (*salvia officinalis*) – forms neatly rounded bushes when regularly picked or clipped. A range of varieties with different leaf colours, such as purple and golden sage, a multi-coloured one called 'Tricolor'. For something different, try pineapple sage, an elegant hardy perennial growing to 90 cm tall with scarlet red flowers.

Thyme – An extremely versatile plant. Many are low, creeping and very useful in general garden planting for softening path edges, growing between stepping-stones or spilling over raised planting areas. They range from variegated silver, golden yellow to deep green and they also flower well with pink or purple blooms in summer. For different flavours, try caraway thyme, low creeping with caraway-scented leaves or lemon thyme, a small bushy plant with a mild lemon flavour.

Rosemary – extremely easy evergreen to grow with blue, lilac or white flowers. There's not a huge difference in flavour so go for one that looks good. 'Miss Jessopp's Upright' can be grown as a 1-m-tall hedge, 'Severn Sea' has a low mounded form whereas 'Prostratus' is a low spreader that is good on dry banks.

Lemon verbena – A tender deciduous shrub that can be grown in pots and brought indoors for winter. Fabulous sherbet scent (worth growing for that alone) and makes a good tea mixed with mint or can be made into a syrup (mixed half with sugar), which is fabulous for cocktails – sounds good, eh?

perennial herbs

Picking perennial herbs regularly will keep them compact and productive. Many flower (the flowers can all be eaten too) and when they've finished flowering, cut them back again to rejuvenate growth. If straggly in spring, clip them hard and feed to generate tasty, fresh new growth for the season ahead.

Chives – Delicious on potatoes and in salads and easy to grow. Sow seed indoors on a windowsill or in a greenhouse into small pots ready to transplant out after frosts have passed, or sow direct when the soil has warmed up. Once established, lift and divide clumps every few years. Try garlic chives in the border, which is a taller, more graceful plant.

Mint – Grow in a pot as it will spread and be difficult to maintain in a border but is ideally repotted or root pruned every year to keep it actively growing. As well as common mint, there are many other interesting alternatives: ginger mint, pineapple mint and peppermint.

Oregano (marjoram) – Golden oregano (*O. vulgare* 'Aureum') works so well in my garden, carpeting the ground at the front of a border and softening the corners of paving. I'd grow it even if it wasn't edible! The wild marjoram has dark green leaves and purple flowers and is another good ornamental. Greek oregano has bristly leaves and full flavour and is great for barbecues but is a little tender. Lots of other varieties too, including sweet marjoram (half-hardy) and pot marjoram.

Annual herbs

Pick them regularly to stop them flowering and seeding, which will also encourage strong new growth.

Basil – A very tender plant. When you buy a pot, it's lots of seeds sown together, and this is the best way to sow. Sow in pots indoors and keep them indoors in full sun or take them outdoors after the last frosts. Sweet basil is the most commonly grown but also try Greek or purple basil.

Chervil – Absolutely delicious with its aniseed-flavoured feathery leaves. It too likes a little shade and a spot that's not too dry. Best sown and protected in autumn as it can go to seed very quickly if it gets too hot and sunny, but having said that, the umbel flowers are rather beautiful, so win-win!

Coriander – A fast-growing herb that can quickly go to seed in hot dry weather. Has long roots and doesn't like transplanting so sow it where you want it to grow and start harvesting when young. Sow every few weeks to keep a succession going as once it goes over it will quickly seed and droop.

Dill – This is worth growing in the border even if you never eat it as it's such a beauty with its yellow umbel flowers and feathery foliage. Very easy to grow from seed. Its aniseed taste is mainly used with fish, but it also works well as a garnish. Cut it as soon as there's enough for a small harvest and it'll regrow. You can let it seed around too, which means you don't even have to sow it and weeding it out is a simple way of cropping it; now that's easy gardening!

French tarragon – Buy a plant or get a cutting from someone as it cannot be grown from seed. It can be slow to establish and easily gets swamped by other plants so perhaps grow in a pot in well-drained compost in a sunny spot. Overwinter in a protected spot.

Lemongrass – Delicious in Southeast Asian cuisine, it's pretty tender so grow in a very sheltered spot and you can get it through a winter by bringing a pot indoors. You can grow from seed but by far the easiest way is to root a stem in a jar of water and then pot up and grow on. It's the easiest way of keeping a succession going over years too. Water well during dry spells. It can get quite tall, around 1.2 m, but be careful of the sharp-edged grass leaves so avoid kids' play areas or where you may brush past it.

Parsley – There are two main types of parsley: curly-leaf and flat-leaf and I think the latter has better flavour but is perhaps less ornamental. Can't make up your mind? Then grow both! They tend to be grown as annuals for best flavour. Sow thinly in pots or ideally sow direct in spring where you want it to grow. Water regularly and replace when leaves yellow and they get tired.

fruit

fruit trees

Picking fruit from a tree and eating it right there on the spot is one of life's great pleasures. A fruit tree will produce for many years to come and, if you don't have much space (or any soil at all to dig into), there are suitable rootstocks to keep them manageable and many that do well in large containers.

Apple (Malus domestica)

There are literally hundreds of varieties to choose from. Grow what you love to eat and some late varieties that store well (see storing home-grown fruit section). Some do better in certain areas so it's worth chatting to growers (they love offering advice). Here's just a few of the vast range out there.

'Cox's Orange Pippin' has a super flavour, juicy and crisp. Better in southern regions.

'Egremont Russet' is a classic, been around for centuries. Nutty, sweet flavour. Good frost tolerance.

'Spartan' has skin that is deep plum red, with almost white juicy flesh. Stays late on the tree.

Some apples are self-pollinating (like 'James Grieve' and 'Arthur Turner'), but most need a pollination partner nearby (one that flowers at the same time). In most towns and cities there'll be enough around (or a crab apple tree that's long flowering and does the job nicely) but if they're not common where you are, plant a partner. These are the four pollination groups.

1 Early flowering (such as Beauty of Bath, Egremont Russet).

2 Mid-season flowering (Cox's Orange Pippin, Epicure).

3 Mid- to late-season flowering (Ellison's Orange, Laxton's Superb).

4 Late flowering (Newton Wonder, Adams Pearmain).

pruning apples

Okay, this will sound technical, but relax and don't get freaked out! The first few (around four) years are mainly training (like kids and dogs) to build up a nice framework and the shape you want (see fruit tree forms section). This mainly means cutting out anything that doesn't work with your shape and taking out weak, damaged or diseased branches and from then on these are the annual basics.

winter pruning for most free-standing apple trees

First, shorten the previous year's growth on each main branch by about one third to an outward-facing bud. This will encourage new branches and spurs and maintain a good shape.

Leave any side-shoots unpruned so they can develop fruit buds the following year, but take off any that will mess up the shape (growing inwards) or rub with others.

Inside the head —
leave leaders alone.
Cut back each lateral
which is growing
into and beyond
the branch leader.

Outside the head —
leave both leaders
and laterals alone

Overcropping and undersized fruit may become
a problem. If this has happened, thin some of
the fruiting spurs and cut out some laterals.

Summer pruning

The main pruning of restricted shapes like cordons, espaliers and fans is done in summer, around the end of August and involves cutting back new shoots (which are stiff and woody with a cluster of leaves at the base) to allow light to reach the fruit to ripen. Cut them back to three leaves above the basal cluster of leaves but leave any new shoots that are less than 20 cm long as they usually have terminal fruit buds (at the end). Remove any upright, vigorous growth completely so you still have a good shape. Take control and make it fit the shape you've got in mind.

CORDONS

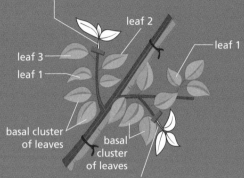

① Cut above third leaf beyond basal cluster.

leaf 2

leaf 3

leaf 1

leaf 1

basal cluster of leaves

basal cluster of leaves

② Lateral side shoot — cut above first leaf beyond basal cluster.

ESPALIERS

① In spring, tie 3 canes to the wire supports as shown.

② In summer, train the growth from the terminal bud and 2 side buds along the canes.

③ In early winter, remove the 2 side canes and lower the branches. Tie them carefully along the horizantal wires. Repeat this training process until the final number of tiers is obtained.

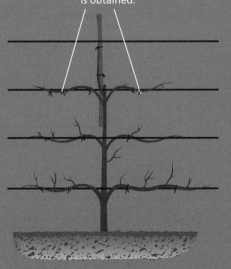

cherry (prunus avium)

Life is a bowl of cherries, or certainly can be. There are many fabulous ornamental cherry trees out there and in the old days most edible sweet cherry trees got way too big for the average garden to be manageable, oh and you also needed two to pollinate each other! Thankfully, many are now self-fertile and can be restricted size-wise with an appropriate rootstock. If you have a nice sunny wall or fence, go for a pre-fan trained on a colt rootstock.

Once the flowers appear, cover with fleece during the night (as they flower early when frosts are still around) and then uncover during the day so pollinators can do their thing. Net the fruit too as it ripens as canny birds will know exactly when they're ready.

Water well while it establishes for the first year and during dry spells until it gets going, but don't drown.

Being a stone fruit, cherries should only be pruned in summer when it's dry to avoid infection of the dreaded silver leaf. Train shapes similar to apples (see above). Prune established standing trees in June to late-July as you would any tree, removing dead, diseased and damaged branches and then, if required, thin to reduce overcrowding and improve airflow.

'Merchant' is an early fruiting, delicious dark cherry but not self-fertile (the early ones tend not to be).

'Stella' fruits in late summer, is reliably self-fertile and a favourite in drier areas (the fruit can split in wetter areas).

'Lapins' is also late summer, very reliable, heavy cropping and self-fertile.

If you only have shade, grow the acid cherry 'Morello' (for culinary use like jams, cakes, tarts and pies), which is also self-fertile.

Fig (Ficus)

I've had some delicious figs over recent years and with climate change we'll probably be growing more of them in the future. Even if they don't fruit that well, the large ornamental leaves smell lovely, and they make a great garden plant for a sunny spot.

To fruit well, they need to be grown in a pot of around 40 cm (it will need to go up a size or two as it matures) as they like to have their roots restricted, or if you grow them in the ground, line a square hole with some old slabs, backfill and plant into that. A pot means you can place it where it'll get most sun too, ideally in front of a sheltered south or south-west facing wall.

Grow it as a small bush or fan it out on wires on a wall (or even grow it up and over a pergola to shade you). Small fruits are formed at the end of summer that develop into next year's crops so ideally protect them from winter frosts with fleece, especially in colder areas.

Water regularly in dry periods, which helps fruit swell, and prune around June (keep bushes nice and open for good air circulation) and take off any unwanted or unripe fruit in September (not the small baby ones for next year!). Repot every two or three years in late winter.

'Brown Turkey' is very popular as it crops well with red, sweet flesh.

'White Marseilles' has white, almost transparent, flesh. They are reliable outdoors and delicious.

Mulberry (Morus)

Mature mulberries are fabulous spreading trees, way too big for the average garden, but perhaps you have somewhere suitable on your estate? The large juicy fruit is delicious too.

Fortunately, a dwarf variety (said to be bred in Japan over 40 years) called 'Mojo Berry' was introduced in 2017 and won RHS Chelsea plant of the year (I was there!).

It's self-pollinating, fruits on new wood and old wood and produces fruit when young, unlike big trees, which can take eight or nine years. It only reaches around 1.5 m in height, is great for a pot and can fruit from late spring to late summer.

When growing in the ground, add plenty of well-rotted horse manure before planting and, when in a pot, a mix of peat-free multipurpose with some added loam (good topsoil), water with rainwater ideally and feed regularly.

Prune to maintain its naturally mounded shape.

pear (Pyrus)

I'd say pears should be eaten when perfectly ripe when they're soft, sweet and juicy (too young and they're crunchy and acidic, too late and they're all mushy!). The window is quite fleeting but there are many pear lovers out there who would put them top of the list.

They are long-lived trees (around 50 years) and prefer heavier soils than light chalky or sandy ones. They are grafted onto rootstocks (see understanding rootstocks). In truth, they are a little more temperamental than apples as they flower a bit earlier (so the blooms are more susceptible to frost) and take longer to fruit well (around 4 to 8 years), but if you have the right conditions and some patience, there should be no stopping you!

Pollination

Pears are likely to need a pollination partner, so you'll need a 'pair of them' (boom boom) or find a neighbour with one (but remember, they are less popular than apples) and try and find out what they've got. There are six groups, with most falling into groups 2 to 4:

- 2 (early flowering), like **'Packham's Triumph'** and **'Louise Bonne of Jersey'**.

- 3 (mid-season flowering), like **'Beurre Hardy'** and **'Conference'**.

- (late-season flowering), like **'Concorde'** and **'Doyenné du Comicée'**.

Pruning: Similar to apples. They can be grown as stand-alone trees or, like apples, trained against a wall as a cordon, fan or espalier and even in a large container.

Varieties

'Conference' are delicious, should be picked just before being ripe and left for a day or two before eating.

'Beth' produces early, yellow-green, small yet delicious fruit.

'Concorde' is heavy fruiting and early and reliable cropping and probably the best for smaller gardens.

Plum (Prunus domestica)

Extremely popular and delicious fruit. Easy to grow and very hardy trees with many varieties including sweet and sour (and then there's damsons, greengages and sweet little Mirabelle plums too, which are all closely related). The flowers appear early in spring, which means they can get frost damaged, which may result in reduced crops and if yours hasn't fruited, that's probably the reason. Some are self-fertile so always produce some fruit but always do far better with another nearby.

They take about five years till cropping although trees grown on the 'pixie' rootstock will reliably produce fruit earlier. It's a good one for restricting growth too and ideal if you want to grow them as a fan on a south-facing wall (which can be easily fleeced for frost protection of the flowers and netted to keep the birds off the fruit).

Pruning: Never prune any stone fruit in winter (as it leaves them prone to silver leaf infection). Prune young trees around March to develop a good shape. In general, prune them like apples aiming for around three to five strong branches. With established trees, prune in summer, around June to late-July on a dry day, keep it to a minimum, removing the 3 Ds (dead, damaged and diseased) branches first.

Varieties
'Victoria' is still the most popular, a classic with sweet yellow-green egg-shaped fruits in August.

'Opal' is rustic and delicious with golden flesh and a small stone that comes away easily.

Both are self-fertile.

peach (prunus persica)

Yes, they can grow well in the UK and are breathtakingly beautiful trees when in bloom, producing delicious fruit if you've got a well-protected south-facing garden or south-facing sunny wall. They certainly do best in mild southern areas and will struggle to crop from north of the Midlands but if you have space and they're not your only fruit tree, they are worth growing for their flowers alone.

Give them as much sun as possible. Plant in moisture-retentive, well-drained soil and grow as free-standing bushes or fan them out onto a wall (which provides extra warmth and frost protection). Fleece flowers in spring to protect from frost and you may need to cover again in summer to protect fruit from birds.

Pollination: They bloom early in the year when pollinating insects are scarce so help them out using a soft brush to gently dab the flowers every couple of days when the flower buds open and keep going till the petals fall.

Varieties
'Peregrine' produces delicious, large, rounded fruit with white flesh.

'Duke of York' fruits end of July, producing fruits with yellow flesh and crimson skin.

Both are self-fertile.

Nectarines can be grown in the UK too, but they are even more delicate and produce less fruit.

peach leaf curl

This can be a real problem, so tackle the minute you see it. Fungal spores land on buds to infest newly emerging leaves in spring, the emerging fungus then feeds on the young leaves, making them distorted and puckered and in turn weakens the plant, leading to the flowers and fruit falling off.

The organic solution is to remove any infected leaves, flowers or fruit as soon as they're spotted. Clear up infected, fallen leaves around trees. Cover wall-trained trees with a polythene sheet in January and February to prevent the fungus developing. Mulch around the base of trees with garden compost to maintain general health, and water well in dry summer weather. Avoid over-feeding with nitrogen fertilisers. Buy resistant varieties.

Quince (Cydonia oblonga)

Quince was a favourite of the Greeks and Romans. The scented golden yellow fruit are too gritty and sharp to be eaten raw, but the jelly (membrillo in Spanish) is delicious with cheese and, when cooked, makes good pie fillings as a companion to apples.

They are gorgeous trees, excellent for small gardens with grey bark, leathery leaves and large open white or pink flowers. They can be fanned onto a warm wall or left as free-standing and are frankly pretty enough even if you don't use much of the fruit.

Varieties
'Vranja' is the most popular and ornamental variety, producing pear-shaped fruits.

'Champion' has large apple-shaped fruit.

Grow in any soil except waterlogged. They are very hardy.

Understanding rootstocks

Dwarfing rootstocks (onto which corresponding fruit cultivars are grafted) have made it easy to find a fruit tree to fit your garden or where you want to grow it (fanned onto a wall, in a pot or as a stand-alone tree). The way to go is to pick a cultivar and then pick the appropriate rootstock, such as 'Bramley M9' (sounds like a classic vintage car!).

Here are the most common rootstocks:
- **Apple:** M27 (approx. 2 m tree), M9 (producing approx. a 2.5 m tree), M26 (producing a 3.5 m tree) or M106 (producing a 4 m to 5.5 m tree).

- **Cherry:** Colt (approx. 3 m tree) or Gisela 5 (approx. 4.5 m).

- **Pear:** Quince A is the most common, producing a tree around 3 m to 6 m, Quince C approx. 2.5 m to 5 m.

- **Plum, damson, peach:** Pixy (2.5 m to 3 m, so good for small fans) or St Julien A (4 m to 4.5 m, ideal for bigger fans or pyramids) and 'Brompton' is vigorous and generally produces a tree up to 6 m tall.

Growing fruit trees in containers

You may think, choose the smallest rootstock for containers, but some are actually too dwarfing. For example, M27 rootstock for apples restricts plants to 2 m and when grown in a pot (which already restricts a plants growth) it's essentially a double dwarfing, which stresses the tree, makes it weak, prone to pests and disease and rarely produces a healthy tree that fruits well. Go the next size up, so in the case of apples, go for an M9.

Most fruit trees like plenty of sun so consider their precise placing before potting up (once potted and watered, it may be too heavy to move!). The size of the container will depend on the size of tree; generally, the bigger the better. Most will require a minimum depth of 40 cm – half barrels work well but do incorporate a drainage layer of crocks or gravel at the bottom (waterlogging is a killer). Use a soil-based compost (such as John Innes No. 3 or equivalent) with some homemade compost/well-rotted manure mixed in to aid moisture retention. Always plant to the soil mark on the trunk so it's the same depth in the ground as it was in the field or previous pot, and some will need staking or some kind of support early on to stop them rocking. A yearly spring mulch with chipped bark, compost or leaf mould makes a big difference too, shading the tree's roots and improving moisture retention. Water thoroughly and regularly in spring and summer (especially when fruit has set) and reduce or even stop watering in winter. From spring onwards, feed every two weeks with a liquid tomato feed or equivalent.

Rootstocks are not required for blueberries and figs.

soft fruit

Blackberry

Let's get berry-tastic! Of
course, the delicious wild
blackberry (bramble) can
be found free of charge
in hedgerows in summer
but is too rampant and
gets way too big for most
of our gardens. There
are many more suitable
garden blackberry varieties,
but you'll still need some
space or ideally make up a

support structure with posts and wires or grow against a
wall or fence to organise them, keep compact and make
them more productive. Thornless varieties can be grown
over arches so you don't snag your trousers on them.

Easy to grow. The flowers open between May and
July (so no frosts to worry about) and fruit is formed
between July and September. Most of these berries like
sun but will still grow well with a little light shade. Water
plants every week or so when establishing, otherwise
only in dry spells.

Pruning: Fanning them onto a structure or wall is
recommended for the less vigorous hybrids. In autumn,
cut down any canes that have fruited that year and then
train and space out new canes onto wires that will fruit
next year (like pruning summer fruiting raspberries).

varieties

'Loch Ness' is thornless and stout so can be grown without any support (and good in pots). Glossy, full-flavoured fruit. 'Karaka Black' has very large fruit with a tangy flavour and is slightly thorny.

Here are some other hybrid berries well worth considering:

- **Tayberry** – a raspberry and blackberry cross. The fruit is red and longer than a raspberry and a little sharper in flavour. Best used for jams and cooking. Early season crop.

- **Loganberry** – another raspberry and blackberry cross. The fruit is long and dark red. Ideal for jams but can also be eaten fresh.

- **Boysenberry** – a loganberry, raspberry and dewberry cross. Thornless. Heavy early season crops of juicy black fruits with a wild blackberry flavour. Needs well-drained soil.

- **Dewberry** – a thorny number! The small black fruits are covered with a grey bloom. Early season crop.

- **Japanese wineberry** – attractive stems with bright red bristles. Mid-season fruit – small, sweet and juicy red.

Blueberry (Vaccinium)

Blueberries are delicious and good for you. There's something special about picking them straight off the bush and sprinkling on your cereal. Kids love them too. As a bonus, their fiery autumn colour is one of the finest in the garden. They do require specific conditions in the ground but are ideal for pots too.

Best in sun but fine in light-dappled shade. In the ground, they require a well-drained yet moisture-retentive acidic soil with a pH of around 4 and 5.5 (the kind rhododendrons thrive in).

If you don't have that soil, grow them in pots using peat-free ericaceous compost with some added leaf mould and if you pot on every two or three years into larger containers, they'll grow into sizeable bushes. They require plenty of moisture, especially when fruit is forming and use rainwater wherever possible (so collect in butts).

Feed pot-grown plants (with liquid seaweed or similar) around once a month until the end of July and harvest when fully blue with a white surface bloom. The fruit is produced on last year's growth so once established, prune in winter to keep an open shape, bearing in mind what is left on the plant is where the following summer's fruit will be produced from.

Some are classed as self-fertile, but they always crop better with another nearby, so I'd buy at least two.

Varieties
'Ivanhoe' – an upright variety with large, dark blue berries. Height and spread up to 2.5 m.

'Bluecrop' – very reliable mid-season cropper. Height 2 m x spread 1.5 m.

'Duke' – an early cropper with firm, fleshy, light-blue fruits. Height and spread 2 m.

They can all be kept smaller in pots.

Gooseberry (Ribes uva-crispa)

Gooseberries can be grown for cooking or eating. Early in the season they are bright green with veining on the skin, delicious in a pudding or gooseberry fool and later in the summer, sweeter varieties ripen (often yellow or red coloured) so delicious eaten raw.

Gooseberry bushes are tough and hardy. They can be grown in the ground in most soils, trained against a wall and also do well in containers. They do like sun. They are very easy to grow, need little attention apart from pruning, which will make a significant difference to their productivity.

Plant bare-rooted plants in winter but not when the ground is frosted. Space bushes around 1.5 m apart if growing more than one (they're self-fertile so don't need a partner) and if grown as single cordons (on a fence, wall or frame), space around 45 cm apart, double cordons 60 cm apart and yes, triple cordons (three upright stems) around 1 m apart. They rarely need watering (except for very dry spells) and mulch the roots annually with organic matter. Feed in spring.

Pruning: Although large uncontrolled bushes will produce some fruit, pruning is key. Here's the basic for bushes, it may sound complicated but is simple – overall, look for a nice open vase shape for air to circulate, and wear gloves (they're spiny things).

First year
In their first early spring of the first year after planting, select five nice main stems and prune them back to around 15 cm. Remove all other stems to the base.

Second year onwards
Around mid-June to July, shorten the current season's growth (the pliable stuff) back to five leaves (except where you want to extend the overall framework). This won't lose you any fruit as it develops mainly on the older wood.

In winter, remove any dead wood, crossing branches and low-lying shoots. Then prune all side shoots by cutting them back to between one to three buds from the base. Shorten branch tips by around a quarter, cutting to an outward-facing bud. Repeat this each year and they'll reward you.

Varieties
'Careless' is a classic with large green berries that can be picked young and cooked or left on to sweeten up and eaten fresh.

'Invicta' is a vigorous variety that needs showing who's boss. A green cooking gooseberry that crops heavily.

Grape (Vitis)

A glass of Chateau Swifty anyone? Grapes can be successfully grown outdoors in many parts of the southern UK already and with climate change we may see them heading further north too. They are vigorous, hardy climbers and most deliver fabulous autumn colour too. Don't get too hung up on the size and taste of the fruit; you can always make fresh grape juice.

Grapes need full sun. Sure, you can grow them in rows like in a vineyard but few of us have the space for that. Grow them on a south or south-west facing wall or over a structure such as an arch or pergola in a protected spot. They will grow on all soils too, except waterlogged ones and are surprisingly hardy plants. Plant in the dormant period between October and March, as long as it's not frosted, and mulch deeply after planting.

Major pruning is carried out in autumn when leafless and any subsequent training, pinching out of shoots and thinning of fruits is done in spring and early summer. There are so many ways to prune and train a grape-vine depending on what you're trying to achieve but my advice is to let it grow to the desired size and height (say, on a pergola?) and once you have a good framework, prune side branches in summer back to around five leaves (taking off excess growth and exposing fruit to the sun to ripen) and then in winter prune side branches back to about two buds.

Some grapes varieties for outdoors in the UK
'Regent' is a large, dark-red, juicy and tasty grape (a popular one in Hackney allotments!) and with a great plummy-red autumn colour.

'Theresa' has sparkly white fruits that are great for the table or wine-making.

'Précoce de Malingre' is an early sweet golden fruit, good for dessert or wine-making.

Strawberry (Fragaria)

Strawberries are the taste of summer. Sure, you can buy them from supermarkets (in and out of season) but home-grown are far juicier and tastier. They are easy to grow, doing well in small spaces and raised beds, containers and hanging baskets. Most produce well for around four years (easily propagated to keep them going) but only fruit for two or three weeks a year so the trick is to grow a few varieties to provide fruit from early summer to early autumn. There are 'perpetual' strawberries that produce all summer, but they are less sweet and juicy and less hardy too. They are best bought and planted annually.

Strawberries like a bright sheltered spot and can cope with a little shade in the day. They need a fertile, well-drained, slightly acidic soil but neutral is fine. When planting in the ground, space them around 45 cm apart in rows of around 75 cm. Add plenty of compost or well-rotted manure a month before and plant on ridges with their roots spread out evenly either side before backfilling. Keep weed-free and water newly planted plants regularly (avoid wetting fruits). When growing in

containers, hanging baskets or growbags, use a peat-free multipurpose compost.

Pick them when they're bright red all over and if they start touching bare earth, use some straw as a gentle pillow beneath to stop them rotting. Birds may be a problem, so keep some netting handy.

The easiest way to propagate strawberries is from runners from a healthy mother plant. Take in late summer but no later than early autumn. They often 'run' themselves, but you can sink a small 9 cm pot filled with multipurpose potting compost beside your strawberry plants and insert individual runners into them. Peg them down with a U-shaped piece of wire. Keep well watered to promote root growth and then cut the new young plants from the parent plant when rooted – simple as that.

Varieties

'Vibrant' produces early season with plenty of fruit and may produce a second flush after a good summer.

'Cambridge Favourite' is a very reliable mid-season strawberry with great flavour. Said to be the best for jams.

'Symphony' is a late-season variety with glossy red fruit.

'Alpine' or 'wild' strawberries (*fragaria vesca*) are smaller, shade-loving plants that produce small, sweetly aromatic fruits and are tough, coping well with cooler conditions. They can be planted directly in flower beds where kids love to hunt for them.

Red and white currants

These produce tart berries ideal for, well, tarts (and pies, jams and wines). They're hard to find fresh in shops these days. They're not sweet enough to eat fresh and are tough plants that grow pretty much anywhere.

They grow well in full sun or semi-shade in any half-decent well-drained garden soil. Ideally, plant bare-rooted plants (from November to March) as long as the ground's not frozen as they are cheaper and generally take better.

Grow them as bushes (space around 1.5 m apart if growing more than one). They can also be grown as vertical cordons, straight up, where space is limited, and you'll get plenty of fruit (up to 1.5 kg) from each cordon. Birds can be a problem; they adore them so keep some netting handy.

Maintain exactly as you would gooseberries when growing as a bush (see Gooseberry).

Varieties
'Red Lake' produces masses of juicy berries on long stems.

'Rovada' ripens late summer and has large berries.

'Blanka' is a white currant producing masses of almost translucent sweet berries in July and August.

Raspberries

Raspberries are my favourite fruit: the taste of summer and early autumn. Summer fruiting varieties fruit in June and July, autumn fruiters from August to October, doing best in milder areas (and when they fruit, it may be a good way of working out what you have inherited).

Site and soil

They thrive in moisture-retentive, fertile, neutral to slightly acidic soils (add plenty of well-rotted manure or compost when plating). Avoid soggy or shallow soils. Plant in a sunny position (although they will tolerate partial shade). If you grow in rows, run north to south to avoid shading each other. Raspberries are self-fertile and pollinated by insects, so avoid a very windy site. Plant

when dormant between November and March.

In containers
They do well in regularly watered containers. Plant single raspberry plants in large containers with 80% multipurpose compost and 20% loam-based potting compost and tie to bamboo canes. Keep the compost moist and feed with a liquid general-purpose fertiliser monthly in summer.

Support
There are many ways of supporting them. A single plant can simply be tied onto a post but the more you grow, the more elaborate a system you may want, with either a post and horizontal wire set-up (to tie them to) or two lines of wires to contain them and tie them to.

Pruning
The easy thing about autumn fruiters is that, once established, you simply cut all the canes down to the ground in February. The new canes will start growing in spring and will bear fruit for you later in the year. Simple as that.

Summer fruiters are marginally more complicated. After picking has finished, cut down all the canes that have fruited and then keep the healthiest looking (around five to ten, depending on size) and tie in and then in February cut just above the top wire to encourage fruit.

Summer fruiters

'Malling Admiral' – great flavour, firm texture and high yields.

'Glen Ample' – high yielding, great flavour, hard to beat.

Autumn fruiters
'Autumn Bliss' – classic and a great cropper. Dark fruits.

'All Gold' – the best of the golden yellow varieties.

care

fruit tree forms

Fruit trees (especially apples, pears and peaches) can be trained in many ways and shapes. They can look fabulously ornamental but there are practical reasons too, as training them uses space efficiently, encourages them to produce more fruit, makes them easier to maintain and pick and when grown against a warm wall, gives shelter so improves fruiting. Think how you live and work shapes into the space you have.

Here are the basic shapes, some can be bought ready trained or you can buy young and train yourself.

Free-standing

Bush: A popular type with an open centre and short trunk around 60 cm from ground level.

Standard: Larger trees with a 2 m clear trunk or half standard with a 1.2 m trunk and all the growth and fruit above. Only suitable for large gardens and a ladder needed for pruning and picking but maybe you just want a lovely tree?

Pyramid: Similar to a bush type but the central leader is left to create an attractive conical-shaped tree. On a dwarfing rootstock, works well in a large container.

Supported: The tree grown either against a wall or fence on wires or onto an independent post and wire structure, which also makes a fine divide in larger gardens.

Cordon: A single-stemmed tree planted at 45 degrees. Unbeatable for growing a range of trees in a small space.

Espalier: The most ornamental as pairs of branches are tied in perfectly horizontally to form tiers (around 45 cm apart). You can buy trees that have already been trained this way.

Fan: Mainly used for cherries, plums and peaches rather than apples, but looks fab. Careful and regular training is important with this shape.

Step-over: Often seen in allotments and small gardens where a single-tier espalier is trained along a wire or structure around 30 cm off the ground, hence the 'step-over', which looks great as an edge or border or along sides of paths.

tools and tool care

Tools are a key part of gardening and a very personal thing. Better quality tools may cost more but last longer (sometimes a lifetime) and tend to be easier, more pleasurable and comfortable to use.

My tool kit consists of:

Hoe: There are lots of differently shaped hoes on the market. I use a long-handled stainless steel Dutch hoe. It needs to be really sharp to cut weeds with minimum work.

Lightweight azada: This is a great tool for doing so many jobs. It's a mini mattock and hoe in one. You can get them in a variety of weights and sizes with the larger ones being ideal for clearing, shaping a plot and creating soil paths, etc.

Leatherman multi-tool: I always have it in my pocket when gardening and use it for everything from cutting string and cable ties to harvesting produce.

Spade and fork: Digging forks and spades are big and heavy, whereas 'border' forks and spades are smaller and far more manageable and ideal once the soil's in decent shape. Stainless steel forks and spades with wooden handles are my favourites as they tend to be lighter, cut through the soil easily and don't hold on to wet clay. They are also simple to keep clean and the handle can be replaced if broken. The blade and neck should ideally be made from the same piece of forged steel. Keeping the spade sharp with a sharpening stone will reduce the effort needed.

Rake: A soil rake is only used to level, break up and refine soil areas. Mine has quite a wide head to cover the soil quickly but use one that feels the right weight for you.

Trowel and hand fork:
Used for hand weeding
and planting small plants
and bulbs. There's a wide
range of shapes and sizes
available but look for a pair
you feel comfortable with.
I particularly like a sharp,

long, thin-bladed hand trowel to dig out deep roots of
perennial weeds and for planting small plants and sets.

Watering can: Metal is more
durable, but heavier than
plastic. A free-flowing and
easy to pour 'rose' is the
most important part.

Secateurs, loppers and saw:
There are many different
designs and price points
for secateurs including
specialist ones for left-
handers. The cleanness of
the cut is all-important so
that any wound will heal

over and stop the risk of disease creeping in. I prefer
bypass secateurs, which cut like scissors, rather than anvil
secateurs, which cut down against a flat surface. Loppers
are basically secateurs with long handles which increase
power and reach, (great for fruit tree pruning). I use a
folding pruning saw for any branches the loppers won't
get through. They tend to work on the 'pull' and give
good control.

Trugs or buckets: Really useful for gathering debris or filling up with compost or harvesting.

Wheelbarrow: Essential in larger gardens and allotments for barrowing compost, etc. I use one with a proper air-filled tyre as I find the

solid tyres difficult to push on uneven ground.

Multi-change kits: There are many multi-change kits with different 'heads' such as a hoe, rake and broom that can be attached to a single handle. They can be very space-saving and perfect for those with storage problems. If opting for this set-up, it's important to buy the best quality you can afford because the joints and fixing mechanism will get more wear than a conventional allotment tool.

String and pegs: For lining plants and rows up.

Cleaning tools: I always use the calm of winter to check over my gardening tools as with a little care they'll perform better and last longer too. First, I clean off any excess soil with a scraper and a wire brush and then use a sharpening stone to sharpen my secateurs, hoe and spade. I use linseed oil on my wooden handles and then some lubricating oil on the metal parts too before hanging up to store.

storing home-grown fruit

Whatever you grow, you'll probably find that at certain times of the year you'll have way too much produce to eat fresh so will need to store it somehow. Apples, quinces and pears are the best for fresh storage. Early apples will only last a few days so cannot be stored, mid-season will last a few weeks and late apples can be stored for months up till mid-spring, depending on the variety and storage conditions. Only store perfect-looking fruit picked from the tree when they are ripe and have good colour. A ripe apple will come away in your hand with a small quarter-turn twist! Use any windfalls for juice, jam or eat straight away.

Traditional apple and pear drying

You'll need a suitable space for storage that's cool, dark yet airy and not too dry. A cool garage or a shed is ideal. A set of trays or shelves (as easy-stacking shelf kits, old orchard boxes, plastic slatted boxes, moulded cardboard trays from greengrocers or ventilated polystyrene containers) that can be stacked on top of each other will save space. Some people wrap each fruit in paper and place folded side down to stop it unravelling but this makes inspection a little tricker. Ideally, stop the individual fruits touching each other and only stack to one fruit high. If you don't have room, only place one layer on another with a layer of cardboard between the two to spread the weight. Label them and check them regularly for rot, throwing away any that show signs.

Drying other fruits

A wide range of fruits such as apples, pears, peaches, plums, apricots, strawberries, blueberries and tomatoes can be dried, stored and used in making cakes, breads, etc. Place in the oven on its lowest setting on a tray and leave the door slightly open. If you catch the drying bug, consider investing in a food dehydrator with trays and a built-in fan, which is ideal for the job.

Freezing

There are plenty of fruits that can be frozen in their fresh state including currants and berries (blackberries, raspberries, blueberries) and are ideal for taking out the freezer for any use or chucking in a nice cool smoothie. Lay them out on a tray initially so they're not touching and put in the freezer. Once frozen, they can be put all together in a freezer bag. Some fruits like plums and greengages can be frozen but are best cooked at a later date, whereas apples and pears are best cooked, or par cooked, first and then frozen.

preserves, jams, marmalade and chutney

Jams are made with mashed fruit and preserves contain whole or large pieces of fruit. Most fruits will make great preserves and jams and are a fine way of using a glut. The key is not to wait until the fruit is overly ripe as it can affect the way they set. High-pectin types of fruit like citrus, apples, cranberries, currants, plums and quince set well so are a good place to start and these high-pectin fruits can be added to low-pectin fruits (like strawberries and cherries) to help them set.

Apples for long storage

● Bramley's Seedling (cooker)   ● Court Pendu Plat (dessert)

● Cox's Orange Pippin (dessert)   ● Lane's Prince Albert (cooking)

● Egremont Russets (dessert)   ● Winter Gem (dessert)

pears for long storage

● **Santa Claus (dessert)**

● **Conference (dessert)**

● **Doyenné du Comice (dessert)**

● **Catillac (cooking)**

storing home-grown vegetables

One full year of growing your own and you'll start to appreciate there are times in the year (such as early spring) when little is produced and other times (mid-summer) when even in a small plot the veggies are coming thick and fast! Anyone who has grown a few will know that gluts are part of the game. Sure, you can give some away to friends and neighbours but it's worth having a plan in place to store your own vegetables for as long as possible.

In clamps

This is a traditional allotmenteer's method of storing root vegetables such as potatoes, parsnips, carrots and swedes on site. Extremely easy to make by simply placing a layer of straw on the ground, stacking the vegetables up and then covering with some more straw and then covering the entire mound with topsoil. On wet and heavy soils, it's worth digging a small trench around the outside at

ground level to drain away any excess water. Crops will store for several months but if there's a prolonged deep frost, some may deteriorate.

In the ground where they grow

We're often so keen to harvest a crop and then wonder why we've got too much of it! Many crops will continue to do well and stay fresh if simply left where they are in the ground and picked or dug up when required. Brassicas (like Brussels sprouts and winter cabbages) can be left for long periods as can root crops (carrots, swedes, parsnips, turnips, etc.) and hardy vegetables like leeks. They're worth checking on occasionally by digging some up and may suffer in extreme wet or frozen conditions.

In a store

If you have a cool frost-free space (such as a cellar, shed or garage) then this is ideal for storing a wide range of vegetables. Set up a shelving system using slatted shelves (to increase airflow and ventilation). Potatoes, squash, pumpkins and mature marrows (see Storing home-grown fruit) can be stored on shelves but make sure they don't touch each other; even the contact with the shelf can cause rotting, so do check occasionally. Some vegetables can be hung in nets or string bags (which helps with ventilation and avoids contact with other objects). Onions, garlic and shallots can be strung up (which is fun) and will last for ages.

Freezing

Many veggies such as corn, peas, broccoli, cauliflower, green beans, squash and winter greens such as spinach, kale and chard all freeze well. Many herbs do too. Some lose their colour and texture when freezing, so consider blanching (boil or steam) before to avoid this. Precise time depends on what you're blanching, but somewhere between one and three minutes should do.

pickles, chutneys and fermenting

As jams and preserves can be made from gluts of fruit, delicious chutneys and pickles can be made from much of your produce that won't last well on the shelf or in the fridge.

Chutney is a combination of chopped fruits or vegetables simmered with vinegar, sugar and spices, reduced to a puree, and lasts for ages.

Pickles are vegetables (and fruits) preserved whole or in chunks in brine or acidic water.

Fermenting is becoming increasingly popular and has health benefits. It is simply adding salt to a vegetable to create a brine within which the beneficial bacteria lactobacillus multiplies and partly breaks down the ingredient to both preserve it and create the tangy flavour.

edible flowers

There are many edible flowers that are fun and help with pollination too.

Types of edible flowers

Calendula (marigolds) come in bright oranges and yellows with a tangy citrus flavour and keep whitefly away (companion planting lesson).

Chive flowers have a strong onion flavour.

Rocket and **nasturtium** flowers have a spicy peppery flavour (maybe too spicy!) and look great either chopped up and mixed in a little or placed on top as a garnish.

Assorted coloured violas, blue borage flowers (cool cucumber flavour), radish flowers, snapdragons, pea flowers and cornflowers (spicy clove flavour) and pinks (floral and sweet) can be picked and used in salads or as a floral garnish.

Almost too pretty to eat!

Groovy Ice Cubes

Kids love this!

Pick edible flowers just before freezing and freeze in water. If you want to get really fancy and can be bothered, freeze them in layers by dripping water over them a little at a time quickly (three layers will do it, leave for a few hours between each) which keeps the flowers pristine. Boil the water first to keep it crystal clear and stop it going cloudy. Use the cubes within a couple of weeks or make a large one with a big mould.

glossary

Annual: A plant that flowers, produces seed and dies in one year.

Bare root: Trees and shrubby plants (like raspberries and redcurrants) can be bought 'bare root' when dormant between November and March. They tend to be cheaper and without soil, so they transport well and often take better too.

Beneficial insect: An insect that benefits your garden by eating or laying its eggs in other insects, thereby controlling their population.

Cloche: Cloches are low portable protective structures made of glass or rigid transparent plastic. Tunnel cloches are low continuous tunnels of flexible plastic. Used to protect (from frost, heavy rain and wind) and extend the growing season both early and late.

Cold frame: An unheated structure (homemade or bought) covered with glass or plastic. Cold frames are used to protect plants from frost and extend the season.

Crop rotation: The planting of a specific crop in a site different from the previous year.

Cutting: A method of plant propagation to make a new plant where a piece of plant leaf, stem, root or bud is cut from a parent plant.

Daisy grubber: A hand held narrow two pronged for like tool ideal for levering out deep roots.

Dib: A loose term used when sowing seed or planting small plants or bulbs into the ground with a 'dibber' (a pointed wooden stick).

Direct sow: To seed directly into the soil instead of starting your seeds indoors.

Foliar feed: A technique of feeding plants by applying liquid fertiliser directly to plant leaves.

Germinate: The beginning of growth in seeds, the action of sprouting, budding or shooting, above the soil. This occurs whenever a plant or seed begins to vegetate into leafy young plants.

Green manure: A crop that is grown and then incorporated into the soil to increase soil fertility or organic matter content. Usually turned over into the soil a few weeks before new planting begins.

Hardening off: The process of acclimatising plants grown under protection – in the greenhouse, for example – to cooler conditions outdoors.

Heavy soil: A soil that contains a high proportion of clay and is poorly drained.

Mattock: A hand tool used for digging and chopping. It has a long handle and a double sided head, one side similar to a pickaxe and on the other a flatter sharp hoe like tool (also known as an adze).

Mulch: Any organic material, such as woodchips, grass clippings, compost, straw or leaves that is spread over the soil surface (around plants) to hold in moisture, improve fertility over time and control weeds.

Perennial: A plant that grows and flowers for years. They are either evergreens or may die back to the ground but will grow again the following season.

pH: A scale from o to 14 that explains the degree of acidity or alkalinity of the water or soil: 7 is neutral, o to 6 is acidic and 8 to 14 is alkaline.

Polytunnel: A tunnel-like structure made of galvanised steel hoops and a polythene cover (like a temporary greenhouse) to extend the growing season and increase the variety of crops that you can grow.

Potager: A potager is a vegetable garden that is also designed and ornamental so is productive but looks great too.

Spit: A spit is a measurement of depth of soil measured by the length of a spades head. One spit is one spade deep, tow is two!

Tilth: Describes the general health and state of the soil. A 'rough tilth' is made by digging and a 'fine tilth' means raked level into small particles for sowing small seed.

index

A

Allium fistulosum (Welsh onion) 125

allotments 7–8

annuals
  herbs 128, 134–7
  weeds 20

apple (*Malus domestica*)
  container grown 160
  drying 192, 193
  forms 180
  freezing 194
  how to grow 140–4
  pollination groups 140–1
  pruning 142
  rootstocks 160
  storage 192, 194, 196
  varieties 140

apricot 193

artichoke
  globe 51
  Jerusalem 52

asparagus 55

aubergine 56

azadas, lightweight 186

B

base dressings 46

basil 134

bay 128, 130

bean(s) 13
  broad beans 58–9
  French beans 12, 60
  green beans 201
  runner beans 16, 34, 63

beds, shaping 12–13

beetroot 30, 64

blackberry 162–3, 194

blood
  dried 45
  see also fish blood and bone

blossom end rot 123

blueberry (*Vaccinium*)
  drying 193
  how to grow 164–5
  preservation 194

borage 205

boysenberry 162–3

brambles 21

brassicas
  Brussels sprouts 68, 199
  cabbage 71, 199
  calabrese 66, 72
  cauliflower 76–7, 201
  and crop rotation 30

coriander 128, 135

cornflowers 205

courgette 12, 30, 82–3

Crambe maritima (sea kale) 126

crop rotation 28–30

cucurbits 30
see also specific cucurbits

cucumber 30, 84–5

currant
preservation 194
red 172
white 172

cut-and-come-again crops 30, 96, 115

Cydonia oblonga (quince) 158, 192, 194

D

damson 160

dewberry 163

digging 16–19
double digging 13, 16
green manures 43
see also `no dig' gardening

dill 136

diseases
clubroot 71
and crop rotation 28
peach leaf curl 157
silver leaf 147

Dowding, Charles 16–18

dwarf rootstocks 160

E

earthing up 107

earthnut pea (*Lathyrus tuberosus*) 124

edible flowers 204–7

espaliers 184, 185

F

Fagopyrum esculentum (buckwheat) 40, 42–3

fans 184

feeding plants 34, 44–6

fennel, Florence 87

fenugreek (T*rigonella foenum graecum*) 40, 42–3

fermentation 202

fertilisers 44–5

fig (*Ficus*) 148

fish blood and bone 45, 46

flame guns 22

Florence fennel 87

flowers, edible 204–7

foliar feeding 46

forks 187, 188

Fragaria (strawberry) 170–1, 193

leatherman multi-tool 187

leek 95, 199

legumes 30, 41, 124
    see also bean(s); pea(s)

lemon balm 128

lemon verbena 132

lemongrass 137

lettuce 30, 96–7

light-excluding materials
    12–13, 18, 22, 42–3

loamy soil 15

loganberry 162–3

loppers 188

M

Malus domestica see apple

mangetout 103

manure 14
    green 40–3
    mulches 18, 19
    poultry 45, 46

marigold (calendula) 204

marjoram *see* oregano

marmalade 194

marrow 82–3, 200

mashua (*Tropaeolum tuberosum*) 127

mint 128, 133

mizuna 96

mulberry (*Morus*) 151

mulches 14, 18, 23, 34

multi-change kits 190

mustard (*Sinapsis alba*) 42–3

N

nasturtium (*Tropaeolum*) 205
    perennial (*T. tuberosum*) 127

nitrogen 44–5
    fixation 30, 41, 124
    `no dig' gardening 16–18

O

onion
    and crop rotation 30
    how to grow 98–9
    storage 20
    Welsh (*Allium fistulosum*)
    125
    see also spring onion

oregano (marjoram) 134
    golden 128

organic feeds 44, 45

organic matter 13, 14–15, 18,
    40

P

pak choi 12, 96

parsley 128, 137

parsnip
    and crop rotation 30

trowels 188

trugs 189

turf, lifting 12–13

turnip 199

V

Vaccinium see blueberry

vegetables
  directory 48–123
  perennial 124–7
  storage 198–202
  see also specific vegetables

viola 205

Vitis (grape) 168–9

W

watering cans 188

'watering in' 46

weedkillers 23

weeds 18, 19, 20–3, 40
  annuals 20
  composting 21–2
  perennial 21
  setting seed 21–2

wheelbarrows 189

whitefly 204

winter greens 201

winter pruning 142

worms 14

Y

yacón (*Smallanthus sonchifolius*) 127